INTRODUCTION

HI! I'm Lillie, the mom in this line-up. I live in the Palm Springs area of Southern California with my husband, Ross, and our four rad kids; Sophia, Mila, Finn, and Knox. My life is busy and wonderful—and sometimes a mess. It's life! But every day is made a little sweeter with good food.

I live for game nights when nobody fights; winter mornings, because our summer ones are torture; and giant dessert bowls while snuggled on the couch next to my (sleeping) husband—religiously—before bed. No kids allowed.

I'm not a registered dietitian or a macro coach. I've always loved healthy foods and working out, but I don't claim to be an expert in nutrition or fitness. I haven't found the secret to chiseled abs year round while eating ice cream sundaes by night and wearing my super-mom cape by day. (Although clearly I have mastered ONE of those things.) I'm just trying to find that sweet spot, where I give enough to myself to feel healthy, happy and READY to give to everyone else I love. Sometimes I feel like I'm nailing it, and other times I'm surviving on four hours of sleep and chronically forgetting to advance the laundry.

Like every mother, I'm busy and pulled in a million different directions, but I believe dinnertime is precious. I think there is joy in prioritizing healthy, delicious meals together—and even more joy if those meals simultaneously help my jeans go on with a little more ease.

I hope you love these recipes as much as we do. And that they help make dinnertime (and jean-zipping) a delight.

xo Lillie

WHY I COUNT MY MACROS

If you're into this stuff.

You certainly don't need to count macros to enjoy this collection of healthy recipes. But, if you do track your food, you can be sure that these meals will be easy to fit and easy to log, as they are all loaded into My Fitness Pal for you.

While I don't think macro tracking is the answer for everyone, it has become my favorite way to maintain a healthy and balanced diet without feeling deprived. When I started counting macros I thought it would be short-lived. I already had a great love of cooking and had been using olive oil as casually as I'd use water. This new perspective—really recognizing the value, or cost, of ALL FOODS—was hard to get behind at first. I was used to the idea of categorizing foods as good and bad, but I was seeing better results than I'd ever seen before, from this mindful, flexible dieting. I was quickly converted. After a few months of diligent tracking, I had totally changed my eating patterns—not necessarily by eating less or even "healthier." I was just learning to be more intentional about what made the cut each day, and making more informed decisions.

Even though logging what you eat can be tedious and time-consuming at first (and it is!), I was loving how I felt physically AND loving what I was eating. All of this made macro counting feel surprisingly sustainable—and sustainability is EVERYTHING.

I was shocked and thrilled to find that I could still be creative in the kitchen, eating foods that I LOVED, all while getting leaner and stronger at the gym. I didn't have that familiar sense of deprivation I'd had when I tried cutting out carbs or sugars or all things processed. I still LOVE whole foods and see so many benefits to a cleaner diet, but I appreciate the balance and perspective that macro counting has given me.

I had seen lots of Instagram accounts boasting the macro-counter's fare, but it wasn't how I liked to eat. I realized quickly this was NOT going to work for me if I had to convert to throwing protein powder in all sorts of concoctions. I hadn't been eating daily waffles and Pop-Tarts® before macros, so I didn't know why I needed questionable high-protein versions now. Hitting protein goals is not a struggle for me (I love meat!), and I'd much prefer extra chicken in my salad to protein powder hiding in my cookies.

Once I stopped trying to count macros the way other people did, I was floored at the satisfying meals and sweets I could eat, all while hitting new goals. I felt compelled to share. I started the Lillie Loves Macros Instagram page, then the *Lillie Eats and Tells* blog, and was determined to eventually get a book out. My goal is to make macro counting manageable for those who might love (and benefit from) it but are overwhelmed by the steep learning curve and logistics.

A daily math puzzle is not for everyone—I get it! Whether you count precisely or think weighing food is for scientists, I hope you'll love the well-balanced and nutritious recipes throughout this book—and that they simplify a healthy, home-cooked dinnertime for your family.

Wanting to know more about macros? I've included a brief section at the end of the book entitled "Macros 101." Remember these are essentially my opinions. Hope they're helpful!

MY FOOD PRIORITIES

QUALITY

I've always loved food. Who doesn't?! I love GOOD, quality food--like a great steak, beautiful seared ahi, fresh burrata, mussels swimming in a bowl of garlicky butter sauce, the darkest flourless chocolate torte! But I also love junk food and still feel a childish pull toward a vending machine, most likely filled with expired Twix® Bars with hard caramel. Like, in that moment, what could be better? I love whole foods, but I also love homemade chocolate chip cookies, and sometimes a handful of my kids' Cheez-Its®, and certainly a Diet Coke®. I can be selective, but I'm not picky. I love FOOD.

When I dove head first into macros, saw results, and fell in love, I knew I had to figure out how to marry this new life with my old one. I was not about to settle for non-oiled skillets full of extra-lean ground turkey mixed with egg whites and a dash of salt. Call me crazy.

There are some who subscribe to the mindset that a healthy relationship with food means you need to "eat to live" rather than "live to eat"--that food needs to be used as fuel and sustenance but not as a source of happiness, reward, or celebration. That might VERY WELL be true for some. Maybe most! And while I support anyone who finds that to work for them, for me food is a beautiful and respectable art form--one I refuse to let die for the sake of my abs.

I see food as a way to enrich your home and comfort and nourish your body and SOUL--as a way to express yourself, to show love, and to bond with people. I think all the best gifts are edible--and somewhere inside my five-foot, ten-inch white-girl body is a little, old Italian lady who spends her days elbow deep in stewed tomatoes and roasted garlic before resting her body and enjoying a big bowl of something sweet.

Do little old Italian ladies finish with a sweet? I don't know. But old Italian Lillie would!

MACROS

As much as I love good food, I also love macro counting and what it's done for me! It's helped me to make and hit new fitness goals and has given me a sense of longevity. It's so freeing not to wonder what new method of weight loss or maintenance I should try, but instead to put that energy into being creative in the kitchen! I've experimented enough to know that I can prepare GOOD-SIZED meals that I CRAVE, while keeping them tightly within my macro budget! This has become an absolute must for me.

My mission in creating and sharing recipes is to help people ENJOY the flavors and variety and quality of GOOD FOOD--while also hitting their goals (and feeling satisfied--maybe even full!) Small portions are easy to make "friendly," but they just make ME UN-friendly. Part of a meal's success for me is getting to eat plenty of it. I'm confident that you'll find that to be true throughout this book.

EASE

It has to be good and it has to be macro-friendly, but I'm not going to make a meal for my family on TOP of that. So it's also got to be family-friendly and DOABLE. That's what these recipes are MADE for. I hope to simplify your life a little bit. You might hate me once or twice while you're dicing veggies for cucumber salsa (I can live with that because it's SO GOOD), but you'll love me when every week you've got quick, lean, TASTY proteins ready to build as many meals as you need. These are easy, flavor-packed meals that will please your family and your fitness pal, AND leave room for a sweet.

LET'S START WITH PROTEIN

Prep just one or two and create a variety of delicious meals all week!

I am not a huge meal-prepper, but that doesn't mean I want to start from scratch every single night! Instead I love to prepare good lean proteins (that reheat well) in bulk, and use them throughout the week as simply or creatively as I choose. This book is set up to help you do the same.

I find having tasty proteins prepped is the KEY to making dinnertime in MY home a breeze. (That's deceiving. I still have children so it is absolutely not "a breeze" but you get it.) If I have to prep and cook my protein along with everything else that goes into a meal, I feel the same sense of panic that comes when I'm supposed to go out and am starting from scratch with my hair--still needing to wash, dry, style--the whole bit!

Hoping someone feels me.

Getting ready to go out is SO much more manageable to me if the hair washing happened YESTERDAY. This allows me to spend my time taming and beautifying the wild mane, instead of sweating under the blow dryer for 20 minutes with a time crunch and a list of female-tasks still looming. Tell me I'm not alone.

Likewise, if I've prepped meat in advance (which itself is painless, as they're all relatively simple recipes,) the rest of the week feels easy. I can spend my time actually being creative with the MEAL, chopping plenty of beautiful fresh veggies and combining things so that the whole is so much greater than the sum of its parts! Rather than tiring of the process and settling for steamed broccoli with grilled chicken (which, I should say, is a recipe for quitting once the weekend rolls around and you feel like you deserve some happiness in your life.) Macro-counting has taught me that there is NO REASON food has to taste boring. No reason.

In this book you'll find four MAIN proteins, with a few variations on most of them. Under the umbrella of each protein are a number of delicious meals to use them in all week.

Each protein recipe is perfect to make in bulk and even freeze if needed. If you're a meal-prep lover, you can package them up in those darling containers. If you prefer to see where the wind takes your cravings each day (like me), here's our plan.

Choose one or two proteins to make for the week. Listed under that protein you'll find several meals that it works beautifully in. Many of them will completely transform the flavor and vibe, so you won't feel like you're eating leftovers every night (because... EW). Alternate your proteins each day, and I promise your family won't even know you're working with a repeat item. You might think you don't like chicken reheated, because you're right! Reheated chicken is gross. But done CORRECTLY and used in the right meals, you won't even know the difference.

You might think you can only make Greek pitas with Greek pork, or obviously you'd only do tacos with the Mexican carnitas. Let go of that. It's not true! You'll be surprised how versatile everything is. Feel free to use what makes the most sense, but don't let the name or a couple of seasonings corner you. TRUST ME.

You also might worry that the macros will vary if you swap meats. I use such low-calorie items in my marinades or add-ins that the macros for each shredded chicken (or each grilled chicken, etc.) are SO similar. Feel free to rebuild the recipe if you want to be precise, but the discrepancies will be so small! I'd give yourself a pass and enjoy the ease.

Let's get cooking.

DISCLAIMER

First, I should make a couple of things clear. I'm not a doctor or a registered dietitian. I'm not a fitness expert or trainer of any sort. All opinions are my own and any macro-tips and info are conclusions I've come to through my research, but they are not hard facts. I have no letters anywhere after my name, but am simply a mom who loves to cook and EAT and count macros. I want to share! I don't have an editing team, unless you count an occasional pre-teen hovering over my shoulder. You will most likely find a mistake here and there. Maybe lots! I hope you'll forgive me.

Many of these recipes are written to "serve one" for tracking purposes. Don't let that deter you from using them for the whole family! With plenty of protein on hand, it's easy to manipulate the meal to serve however many you need!

GROCERY STAPLES

A list of things you'll find in my kitchen, which probably means you'll find many of them in these recipes!

TRADER JOE'S®

Sweet Onion Bacon Vinaigrette: A great bottled dressing.

Green Goddess Salad Dressing: Great for salads and wraps.

Spicy Peanut Vinaigrette: My FAVORITE for any Asian salad.

Arugula: For some reason theirs is my favorite.

Tomato basil hummus: A great lower fat hummus.

Tzatziki: For Greek pitas or bowls.

Avocado tzatziki: A new Tzatziki option that's even better!

Healthy ham: Zero fat which can come in handy.

Fat-free cottage cheese: for when I want fat-free. RARE.

Fat-free feta: A staple for all things Greek.

Three cheese lite Mexican blend: Favorite for Mexican meals.

Toscana cheese soaked in syrah: So good. Not macro-friendly.

Lite mozzarella: For pizzas.

Honey goat cheese chevre: Spread on burgers/chicken.

Dry toasted slivered almonds: Best almonds! Keep in freezer.

Maple Donut One® Bars: Best price I've found. Only flavor I like.

Queso: So low in fat. I love to throw it on my lavash nachos.

Chipotle Black Bean Dip: As a base for Mexican pizzas.

Salsa Verde: Used in lots of recipes like carnitas.

San Marzano tomatoes: The best canned tomatoes ever.

Tomato paste: Sold in a tube which is so helpful for storing!

Rustica marinara sauce: If you can't get Costco's Victoria.

Olive oil spray: Especially for when I need just a spritz on salad.

Jarred bruschetta: A little can go a long way to top a dish.

Balsamic glaze: Drizzled on pizzas and salads. A MUST.

Fig butter: Always on our burgers.

Bottled red enchilada sauce: For enchiladas and chilaquiles.

Sweet Chili Sauce: Slightly lower in carbs than most.

Green Dragon Hot Sauce: Really good for eggs and Mexican food.

Yuzu Hot Sauce: Fresh and zesty hot sauce.

Farro: My favorite chewy grain for salads. Easy to cook.

Cornbread mix: Not macro-friendly. But a family favorite.

Semi-sweet chocolate chunks: For variety in chocolate chip cookies.

Everything bagel seasoning: Always on sandwiches/wraps.

Frozen brown rice: So easy. The only rice we use.

Frozen mahi burgers: GREAT for a quick meal. Taste and macros.

Frozen Dorot® garlic cubes: An absolute MUST!

Sweet-potato fries: Theirs are SO good. A family favorite.

WALMART®

Brioche hamburger buns: Best price for these perfect buns.

Extra- Thin Mission® corn tortillas: For all of my tacos and tostadas.

Joseph's lavash AND pitas: Absolute must while watching carbs.

FlapJacked Double Chocolate Mighty Muffins: For dessert bowls!

Purely Elizabeth granola: To top yogurt or dessert bowls.

Hughes sugar-free bbq sauce

COSTCO®

French bread loaves: You can slice thin for paninis.

Ground turkey: Burgers, bolognese, chili, tacos.

Packaged rotisserie chicken: Mostly just for soup. Weird alone.

Pork tenderloin: A staple for us. Inexpensive, lean protein.

Shaved parmesan: To top salads and all things Italian.

Pesto: An easy staple for my kid's pizzas, sandwiches, pasta.

Ziploc® Bags

Jimmy Dean® Turkey Sausage Links: For breakfast sandwiches.

Pre-cooked bacon: The only bacon we buy! It's great.

Frozen chicken tenderloins: Much more tender than breasts.

Frozen shrimp

Don Lee Farms® Chicken Patties: Great macros and flavor.

Panko breaded chicken tenderloins: Great for fam. Decent macros.

Knudsen Low-Fat Cottage Cheese: My FAVORITE. A staple.

Kirkland® Organic Peanut Butter: Stir then store in pantry to drizzle.

Canned tomatoes: For soups and chilis.

Victoria® Organic Marinara: Best jarred marinara for macros.

Boxed chicken stock: For soups and chilis.

Papa Pita: For the kids' flatbreads when I use Joseph's

FITCRUNCH® Bars: Second favorite bar to G2G. Great macros.

BASIC GROCERY STORE (For me it's Stater Bros.®)

Lots of this is also at Walmart

Fresh bolillo rolls: Hollow-out for sandwiches.

Kaiser buns: Hollow out for burgers.

Rice cakes: Plain and tomato basil are my go-to for topping for snacks.

Better Oats Instant Oatmeal: A lower-carb oatmeal.

Canned green enchilada sauce: For soups and chilis.

Canned green chilies

Canned chipotle peppers in adobo: For chipotle cream!

Apple cider vinegar: For pickling onions.

Stubb's® bbq sauce: Lower in carbs--for pulled-pork sandwiches etc.

Walden Farms Maple Walnut Syrup: Love it to sweeten cottage cheese.

Fresh chicken breasts: When on sale. For instant pot or skewers.

Extra-lean ground turkey 99/1: You can also ask them to grind some.

Fat-free(or lite) sour cream: For Chipotle cream and basil aoili.

Greek cream cheese: Love this. Can't find? Just use reduced fat.

Bolthouse® Cilantro Avocado: When we're out of home-made.

Bolthouse Classic Ranch: For basic ranch needs.

Dannon® Light & Fit Greek yogurt: We love vanilla.

Califia® Farms almond milk: Toasted coconut is my favorite.

Califia Farms creamer: All flavors are good for protein shakes.

Fat-free Fairlife® milk: Mostly for cooking.

Fat-free Reddi Whip®: I keep bottles stocked for dessert bowls.

Cotija cheese: Always on Mexican food. A little goes a long way for flavor.

Treasure Cave® reduced-fat blue cheese: For burgers, pizzas, and salads.

Laughing Cow® Spicy Pepper Jack Cheese: Favorite flavor by far.

French's® Honey Mustard: On my daily crunch wrap.

Basil paste: In tube in produce section for basil garlic aioli.

Newman's Own® Sesame Ginger: Love this light option in Asian salads.

Columbus® Maple Syrup and Honey Turkey Breast: For crunch wraps.

Jennie-O® Oven Roasted Chicken Breast: For sandwiches.

Jarlsberg® lite Swiss Cheese: Sliced extra thin from the deli.

Dorot garlic cubes: If you didn't get yours at Trader Joe's.

Frozen cauliflower rice: Fresh works, but this way you can stock it.

Frozen diced onion: So easy to cook with.

Halo Top®/Enlightened®/Arctic Zero®: Low-carb/high-protein ice cream.

Dreyers® Slow Churned: Really good, and close in macros to those above.

Produce I always keep stocked: Bananas, strawberries, pears/peaches/or mangoes, spring mix, arugula, red onion, tomatoes, bell peppers, fresh basil in a pot, lemons, limes, and cilantro.

Produce I often keep on hand: Apples, blueberries, spaghetti squash, delicata squash (when in season), butter lettuce for sandwiches, romaine for tacos, cherry tomatoes, cucumbers. white onion, fresh mint in pot, broccoli, cauliflower florets, and zucchini.

ONLINE

G2G Bars: My favorite protein bars. My affiliate code "Lillie" saves 20%*

Dymatize® ISO 100 Chocolate Peanut Butter: Favorite protein powder!

Peach or lemon vinegar: Lots on Amazon®. I use as dressing for my salads.

Cut Da Carb: My FAVORITE low-carb wraps for daily crunch wraps.

Joseph's: If my Walmart is out.

Flapjack double chocolate mighty muffins: If Walmart is out.

* If you order the G2G bars with my affiliate code, I will earn a small commission. But I'm linked with them because they are indeed, my FAVORITE bar.

CONTENTS

Protein recipes are marked with an asterisk. Use those proteins all week long in the variety of recipes listed below it.

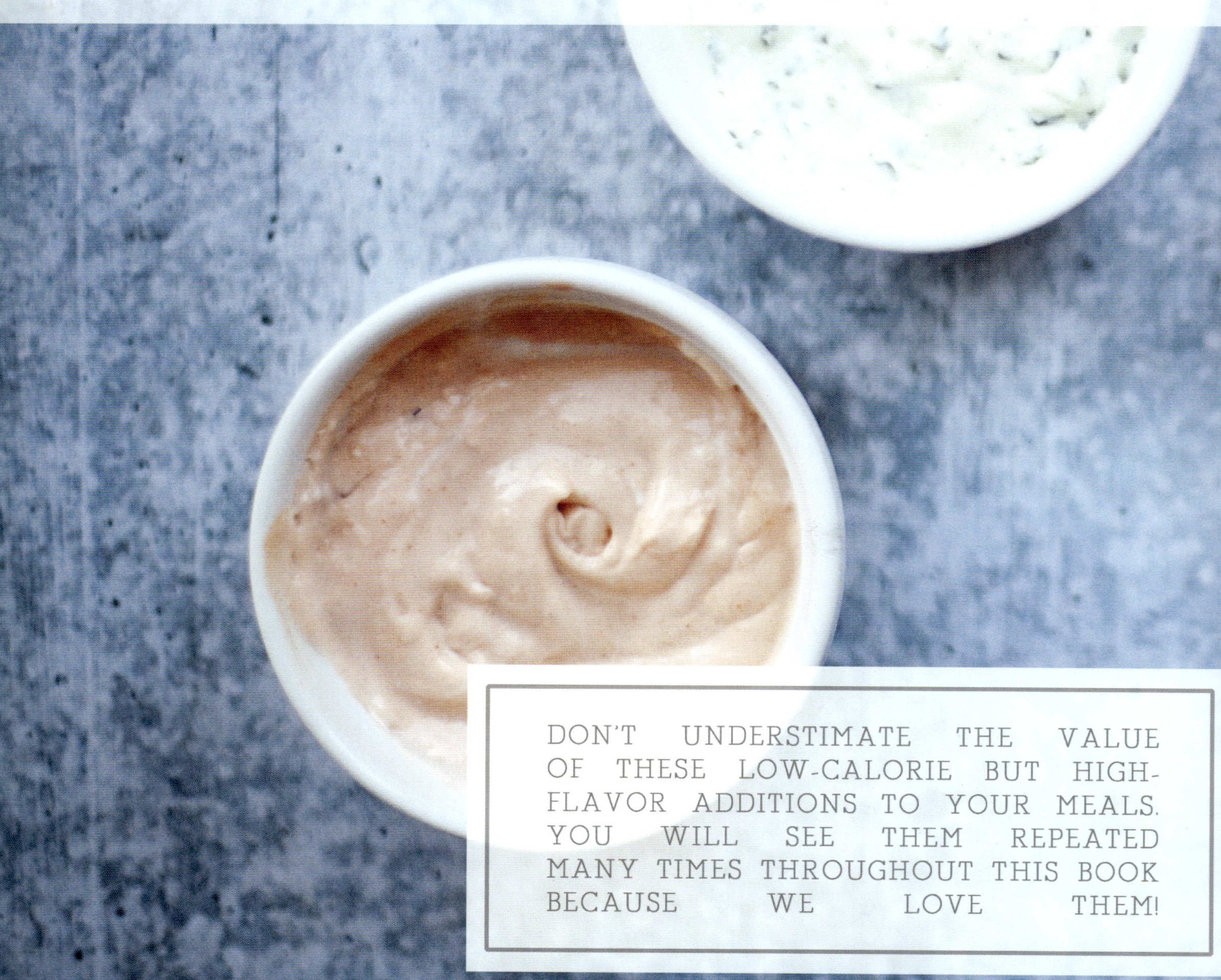

STAPLE SAUCES AND FLAVOR-MAKERS

light basil garlic aioli

. . . .

2 frozen Dorot garlic cubes
2 frozen Dorot basil cubes (or 2 tsp basil paste)
1/2 cup fat-free sour cream
Pinch of salt and pepper

Thaw cubes and mix it all together!

NOTES:

This is so incredible on any grilled sandwich, hamburger or wrap!

Frozen cubes: May use 2 cloves of minced garlic and 2 tsp of fresh minced basil instead.

Sour cream: For both spreads, reduced-fat sour cream works great, of course, as well as Greek yogurt or light mayo. I just prefer the consistency and mild flavor of the sour cream. If you use a different base, just log the sour cream or mayo, the other additions are nearly negligible anyway.

. . . .
NUTRITION
. . . .

Serving size: 30 g (2 Tbs)
27 Cal/0F/4.8C/0.9P

Search MFP for:
"Lillie Eats and Tells Light Basil Garlic Aioli"

skinny chipotle cream

. . . .

1 cup fat-free sour cream
2 chipotle peppers from the can
1 Tbs adobo sauce from the same can

Spoon 1 cup sour cream into a small food processor, or blender jar. Add about 2 chipotle peppers plus 1 Tbs of the sauce (depending on how much heat you like) to the sour cream and blend or process.

NOTES:

Chipotle peppers in adobo sauce : Found at most grocery stores near the green chilis and enchilada sauce. I prefer the Embasa® brand.

If you're worried about not using the entire can of the chipotle peppers, you can blend up the whole thing and keep it in your fridge. Then, just mix together a few tablespoons of the sour cream and a little chipotle pepper paste as needed! Feel free to add some lime juice and salt. It will last for 7-10 days in the fridge. The truth is, I just keep mine until it's weird and watery!

You can see throughout the book, and on the *Lillie Eats and Tells* Blog, that we eat this on EVERYTHING. Easily my favorite low-cal condiment.

. . . .
NUTRITION
. . . .

Serving size: 30 g (2 Tbs)
28 Cal/0.3F/4.5C/1.7P

Search MFP for:
"Lillie Eats and Tells Skinny Chipotle Cream

pico de gallo

2-3 roma tomatoes, diced (scoop out seedy
   insides with your fingers first) (240 g)
1/2 a small red or white onion, diced small (140 g)
1 bunch cilantro, chopped (20 g)
1 jalapeño, diced (30 g)
1/4 tsp or so of kosher salt (more if needed)
1 lime, juiced

Combine in a bowl!

Serving size: 60 g
12 Cal/ 2.4C/0F/0.6P-- pretty much nothing

lightened-up, creamy cilantro-lime ranch

PREP: 5 MINUTES   **TOTAL:** 10 MINUTES   **SERVES:** 10

1 packet of ranch dressing mix (1 oz)
1 cup light mayo
1 cup fat-free milk (add more if it's too thick)
¼ cup salsa verde
1-2 jalapenos seeded
2 cloves of garlic, minced (or frozen cubes)
1 whole lime juiced (about 2 Tbs)
½ cup packed cilantro

NOTES:

Mayo: I use Best Foods®, with a green label, which only has 1 gram of fat per serving for these macros. I'm sure you could use Greek yogurt if you feel better about that.

Milk: I use Fairlife which has the lowest carbs.

This makes a huge batch. Feel free to cut in half. Or, we like to make a big batch and freeze it in plastic ramekins from Smart & Final® for constant replenishing since we fly through it. It is thinner when thawed from the freezer. If that bothers you, don't double it.

No time for homemade? Bolthouse Cilantro Avocado is a good store-bought alternative. But we prefer this one and the macros are BETTER!

NUTRITION

Serving size: 30 g (2 tbs)
21 Cal/0.7F/2.8C/0.8P

Search MFP for:
"Lillie Eats and Tells Lightened Up Creamy Cilantro Lime Ranch"

1. Blend all ingredients in a blender or food processor until smooth. Place in fridge for an hour if you have time. No big deal if not.

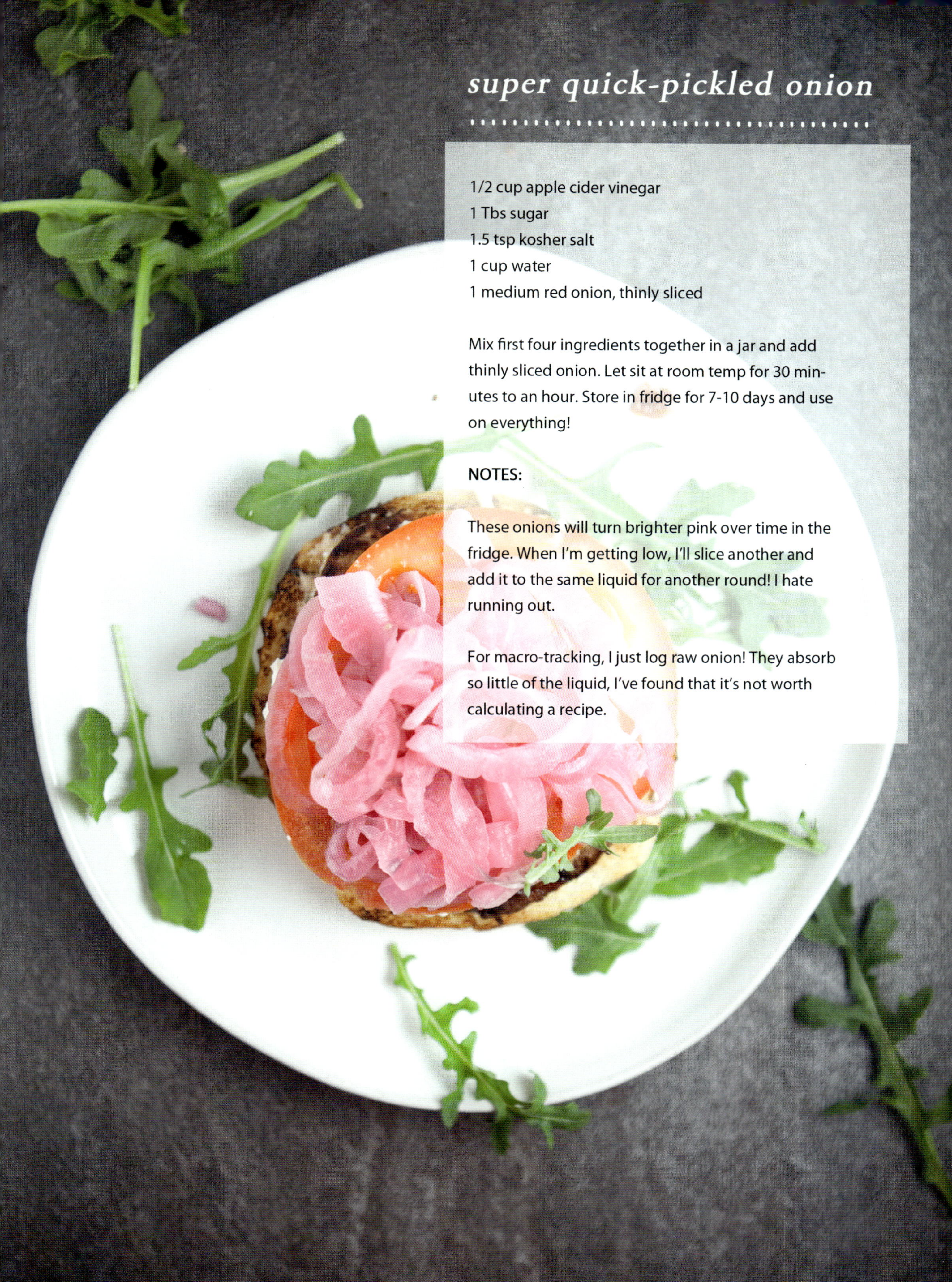

super quick-pickled onion

1/2 cup apple cider vinegar
1 Tbs sugar
1.5 tsp kosher salt
1 cup water
1 medium red onion, thinly sliced

Mix first four ingredients together in a jar and add thinly sliced onion. Let sit at room temp for 30 minutes to an hour. Store in fridge for 7-10 days and use on everything!

NOTES:

These onions will turn brighter pink over time in the fridge. When I'm getting low, I'll slice another and add it to the same liquid for another round! I hate running out.

For macro-tracking, I just log raw onion! They absorb so little of the liquid, I've found that it's not worth calculating a recipe.

INSTANT POT (OR SLOW COOKER) SHREDDED PORK TENDERLOIN

salsa verde crispy carnitas

PREP: 30 MINUTES   TOTAL: 2-6 HOURS   SERVES: 10-12

2-3 lbs pork tenderloin
Seasoned salt
16-oz. jar Herdez® or other salsa verde
8 cloves of garlic, minced (or frozen cubes)
1 medium white onion, diced (250 g)

NUTRITION

Serving size: 100 g shredded carnitas
141 Cal/2F/7C/22P

Search MFP for:
"Lillie Eats and Tells Easy Low Fat Crispy Slow Cooker Carnitas"

1. Trim fat off meat and pat dry. Cut into chunks, 3-4 inches long. (This helps the pieces be shorter later like carnitas.) Season liberally all over with season salt and sear on all sides (in a couple of batches, if needed) with the saute setting in your instant pot.

2. Cover with salsa, garlic, and onion. Seal lid and vent, press manual, and set for 45 minutes on high. When it's done, let it naturally release for 10-15 minutes, then open the vent, and then the lid, when it lets you easily.

3. When done, shred it and toss it around in the juices. I like to pull out my chunks and shred them in a new dish, then pour a little more than half of the liquid over it and toss it around in those juices.

For Slow Cooker, sear in a hot pan on the stove, then move to a crock pot and cover with the salsa, garlic, and onion and cook on high for 4-6 hours (or until tender.)

P.S. You can use the meat like this, and the macros are accurate, BUT to make it EXTRA delicious, with some crispy pieces that are more like authentic carnitas, crisp up as much as you need in a hot fry pan or broil on a sheet pan. This is a MUST! It reduces some moisture and brings out SO much flavor and texture. I store the bulk of it straight out of the instant pot, but crisp up what we need for that meal.

When you fry the meat it will shrink down, but you still get the macros from your full portion. For accuracy, weigh out your portion before you crisp it up. Or, weigh your batch before and after you fry/broil it to calculate how much it shrinks (if you want to account for it.)

*This recipe was adapted from my friend Sarah DeVore!

shredded greek pork

PREP: 30 MINUTES   TOTAL: 1–6 HOURS   SERVES: 10–12

2-lbs pork tenderloin, chopped into 3-inch long chunks
Seasoned salt (or regular kosher salt will work)
1 medium sized onion, diced (270 g)
1 red bell pepper, diced (115 g)
8 cloves garlic, minced (or frozen cubes)
Juice from 1 lemon
1/4 cup juice from pepperoncini jar (optional)
1 tsp dried oregano
1 tsp lemon pepper
1 tsp kosher salt
1/2 tsp pepper
Parsley (optional)

We love to do a double batch and use the whole two-pack. I'll never complain about too much Greek pork in the fridge!

....

NUTRITION

....

Serving size: 100 g shredded Greek pork
125 Cal/2.2F/4.5C/20.8P

Search MFP for:
"Lillie Eats and Tells Shredded Greek Instant Pot Pork"

1. Trim fat off meat and pat dry. Cut into chunks, 3-4 inches long. (This helps the pieces be shorter later like carnitas.) Season liberally all over with season salt and sear on all sides (in a couple of batches, if needed) with the sauté setting in your instant pot.

2. Turn instant pot off, add finely chopped onion and bell pepper. Add back in the pork, the pepperoncini juice, garlic, lemon juice, oregano, lemon pepper, kosher salt, and pepper. Turn your pot to manual (high pressure), then up to 50 minutes. Close the lid and seal the vent!

3. Allow to naturally release. Then open and shred, tossing in juices. Add a fresh squeeze of lemon juice and a big pinch of parsley (optional and mostly to make it pretty!)
Just like my favorite carnitas recipe, I strongly suggest you broil the cooked meat, or fry it up with a little cooking spray over high heat before serving. It's one more step, but it only takes a few minutes! It reduces the moisture and TOTALLY magnifies the flavor and makes it yummy and a little crispy. It also keeps your pitas from getting soggy. I always keep some of the juices in the Pyrex® I'll store my leftovers in, so I can bring it back to life if we don't eat it all and it seems too dry later.

4. When done, shred it and toss it around in the juices. (I like to pull out my chunks and shred them in a new dish, and then pour a little more than half of the liquid over it and toss it around in those juices.)

For Slow Cooker, sear in a hot pan on the stove, then move to a slow cooker and cover with the rest of the ingredients. Cook on high for 4-6 hours (or until tender.)

....

P.S. Crisp up as much as you need in a hot fry pan or broil on a sheet pan. This is a MUST! It reduces some moisture and brings out SO much flavor and texture. I store the bulk of it straight out of the instant pot, but crisp up what we need for that meal.

When you fry it, it shrinks down, but you still get the macros from your full portion. So, weigh out your portion before you crisp it up for accuracy.

....

bbq pulled-pork

PREP: 30 MINUTES　　TOTAL: 50 MINUTES　　SERVES: 5

2-lbs pork tenderloin
1 Tbs liquid smoke
1/2 cup water
1 whole chopped onion (280 g)
8 cloves garlic (or frozen cubes)
1 Tbs brown sugar
2 tsp dry mustard
2 tsp onion powder
1 tsp chili powder
1 tsp cumin
1 tsp paprika
1 tsp kosher salt
1/4 tsp pepper

NOTES:

Pork tenderloins: I buy mine at Costco.

Liquid Smoke: Sold at grocery stores near the bbq sauce.

NUTRITION

Serving size: 100 g Cooked Pork
119 Cal/2F/3C/21P

Search MFP for:
"Lillie Eats and Tells Bbq Pulled Pork"

1. Turn instant pot to sauté and let it heat up while you trim fat off pork, pat dry, and cut into 4-inch chunks.

2. Sprinkle pork chunks liberally with season salt, and place in hot instant pot to sear for a couple of minutes on each side. Then, turn instant pot off to stop the sauté setting.

3. Add in the rest of your ingredients and combine a little. Push the "manual" button, setting it for 45 minutes at high pressure. Close the lid and the pressure valve. Now, go put your feet up.

4. Allow for 10-15 minute natural release, then open the vent, and eventually the lid (when it doesn't fight back.)

5. I like to pull out the chunks and shred them in a shallow dish for ease. Then, pour as much of the juices from the pot over it as seems good. Toss it around. Don't worry about the macros from the leftover juice. It's seasoning and water. Just mix in as much as you can to get it nice and distributed through the meat. I work in more than you'd think.

P.S. If you like your pork a little less juicy and more crispy, you can fry some up in a pan with cooking spray like carnitas. Or, broil it for ten minutes on a sheet pan. We like it both ways. Just weigh your portion before as it will shrink, which increases its macros for 100 grams.

For Slow Cooker: Set to high for 6 hours or low for 8-10. When done, shred with two forks and toss around in the juices.

Feeding the family: I hope you are! This is an easy winner.

Meal-prep thoughts: I like to use the whole double pack from Costco and double this recipe since it works in so many meals and freezes great.

homemade tostadas with salsa verde carnitas

PREP: 20 MINUTES   TOTAL: 30 MINUTES   SERVES: 1

3 Extra-Thin Mission corn tortillas
Fat-free refried beans (25g)
Salsa verde carnitas (130 g)
Shredded lettuce
1/4 cup pico de gallo (60 g)--pg 13
Mango, diced (20 g)
1/4 of an avocado, sliced (30 g)
Cilantro
1 Tbs skinny chipotle sour cream (15 g)-- pg 12
1 Tbs creamy cilantro-lime ranch (15 g)--pg 14
1 tsp cotija cheese (5 g)
A squeeze of lime

NOTES:

Tortillas: I find the "extra-thin" tortillas at Walmart and Ralph's. If you can't find them, just account for a few more carbs overall (if you still eat three). The "extra-thin" tortillas are 8 carbs a piece.

Beans: This calls for just about 1/2 Tbs of beans per tostada. Feel free to add and log more if you like! I use just a tiny bit to keep my carbs down.

Pico de gallo: You can always grab a store-bought if you'd like. Macros are all very similar. (Like 3-4 carbs for 60 grams.)

Cotija cheese: This adds so much authentic flavor to Mexican food. Look near any other mexican cheeses or creme. If you can find it, sub with crumbled feta.

Dressing: If you're in a pinch, sub Bolthouse Avocado Cilantro for the ho me-made cilantro ranch.

1. Spray a medium-hot pan with cooking spray. Spray your "extra-thin" thin mission tortillas with a quick mist as well, and sprinkle with kosher salt. Cook until nice and crispy on each side--Just took a few minutes. Let rest on a paper-towel lined plate. (I didn't use mine for like an hour, and they were great! So, no rush here. You can even make them ahead!)

2. Now, top three tostadas with a VERY thin layer of re-fried beans, carnitas, and cotija cheese.

3. Bake at 400 for a few minutes--just long enough to warm it all back up and liven up the cotija a little.

4. Remove from oven and top all three with: lettuce, pico, mango, avocado, cilantro, homemade fat free chipotle sour cream, and cilantro lime ranch. (Divide amounts by the three tostadas.)

P.S. I put a cookie sheet on my scale with my three shells. Then, add topping and tare (zero out) between each addition. Quick and easy.

Feeding the family: I love tostadas because I can have them built for my whole family and ready to go in the oven at the same time. I can have mine weighed and measured, so I just have to add the cold toppings during the dinnertime chaos. It's a little smoother than tacos. And usually I'll just use the store-bought tostada shells for my kids because they don't know the difference!

NUTRITION

Serving size: 3 decked out tostadas
463 Cal/13F/49C/38P

Search MFP for:
"Lillie Eats and Tells Tostadas with Carnitas"

our favorite carnitas tacos

WITH FRESH MANGO AND CILANTRO-LIME RANCH

PREP: 15 MINUTES   TOTAL: 20 MINUTES   SERVES: 1

3 Extra-Thin Mission corn tortillas
2 Tbs skinny chipotle cream (30 g)--pg 12
Salsa Verde Crispy Carnitas (130 g)
Avocado, sliced (20 g)
Mango, diced (25 g)
Onion, diced (10 g)
Spring mix
2 tsp Tbs cotija cheese (10 g)
2 Tbs light cilantro-lime ranch (30 g)-- pg 14
Radishes, cilantro, etc...

NOTES:

Tortillas: I get the "extra-thin" tortillas at Ralph's®
and sometimes Walmart. Only eight carbs per tortilla
and they're totally normal-sized, not tiny like street
tacos. If you use another tortilla, just factor in the few
extra carbs, if you track.

Cotija: I think it's the secret to bringing Mexican food
to life with so little fat!

NUTRITION

Serving size: 3 tacos
495 Cal/13.4F/51.4C/42.2P

Search MFP for:
"Lillie Eats and Tells Carnitas Tacos"

1. Heat leftover shredded carnitas with some of its
juices in a hot skillet sprayed with cooking spray to
crisp up.

2. In another pan, cook tortillas over medium-high
heat, spraying each side with cooking spray.

3. Divide everything between the three tortillas. Top
each with a thin spread of chipotle cream, carnitas,
avocado, diced mango (if you have it), red onion,
spring mix, cotija, and a drizzle of cilantro lime ranch.

P.S. This is the simplest and most obvious thing to do
with the carnitas, but probably my favorite.

quick and light tostada pizza
WITH CRISPY CARNITAS

PREP: 5 MINUTES   TOTAL: 12 MINUTES   SERVES: 1

1 Joseph's Pita
1 Tbs Trader Joe's Chipotle Black Bean Dip (15 g)
2 tsp low-fat Trader Joe's Mexican cheese blend (10 g)
1/4 cup instant pot carnitas (60 g)
Romaine or iceberg lettuce, finely chopped
2 Tbs pico de gallo (25 g)--pg 13
1 Tbs guac or sliced avocado (15 g)
1 Tbs fat free-sour cream or greek yogurt (15g)
1 tsp cotija cheese (5g)
1 Tbs lightened up cilantro-lime ranch (15 g)--pg 14

NOTES:

Pitas: Found at most Walmarts now, and always on Amazon.

Black bean spread: You can sub 1 Tbs refried beans mixed with 1 tbs favorite jarred salsa. The macros will be close enough.

Pico de gallo: Usually I'm making these for lunch after we've had Mexican for dinner and there's leftover pico lying around. But feel free to use store-bought.

Cotija: If you can't find cotija, feta is a good alternative. If you don't think you like cotija because it stinks, try again! It is SO KEY to Mexican food in my opinion.

Cilantro-Lime Ranch: Sub Bolthouse Cilantro Avocado if you're short on time.

NUTRITION

Serving size: 1 pizza
265 Cal/8.8F/23.8C/26.3P

Search MFP for:
"Lillie Eats and Tells Quick and Light Crispy Carnitas tostada pizza"

1. Heat oven to 425. Spread black bean dip on the pita, then top with shredded cheese and carnitas. Spray with a mist of cooking or olive oil spray and and sprinkle with kosher salt.

2. Bake on a pizza pan (or cookie sheet) for 5-8 minutes until edges are browned and crispy. Top with lettuce, pico, avocado, sour cream, cotija, and dressing. Maybe eat two because they're SO LIGHT.

P.S. I know that not everyone is able to get specific brands, but these are the brands I used for these specific macros. For the most part, the macros will be the same if you find any light shredded cheese blend when we're working with this small amount.

If you track your macros, you can log everything individually to be precise (if your brands are different). Or, you can log mine and call it good.

This is an easy meal to get added protein. I'd love to pile this high with twice the carnitas if I had room. If you struggle to hit your protein, keep your meats lean and double them up in recipes!

Feeding the family: My family love these! If yours does not, pull out the freezer stash of mozzarella and pepperoni.

Meal-prep thoughts: These should bake up just fine if assembled ahead of time. Fry your pork first, so it doesn't make the pita soggy. You can cook over medium heat in a pan until crispy and cheese is melted.

greek pork pitas

WITH CUCUMBER SALSA, HUMMUS, AND TZATZIKI

PREP: 30 MINUTES   TOTAL: 35 MINUTES   SERVES: 1

For the Pitas
2 Joseph's pitas (Walmart or Amazon only)
2 Tbs lower-fat hummus (30 g)
3.5 oz Greek pork OR carnitas (100 g)
2/3 cup cucumber salsa (see recipe below) (150 g)
Butter lettuce, chopped
2 Tbs tzatziki (recipe below)
Fresh squeeze of lemon
A pinch of fresh mint

For the Cucumber Salsa (serves about 8)
2 cups cucumber, diced (250 g)
2 cups firm roma tomatoes, diced (250 g)
1 small red onion, diced (150 g)
1 cup red bell pepper, diced (120 g)
1 Tbs olive oil
1/4 cup fat-free feta
1/4 -1/2 cup fresh mint (depending on taste)
Big pinch or two of kosher salt
Fresh ground pepper to taste
1 lemon, juiced

For the Tzatziki (serves about 8)
1 cup non-fat Greek yogurt
3 cloves of garlic, minced (or frozen cubes)
1/2 English cucumber, grated/squeezed/drained
1 Tbs fresh mint, chopped (or dill)
2 Tbs fresh lemon juice
1/2 Tbs olive oil
1/4 tsp sea salt
1/4 tsp freshly ground black pepper
3-4 Tbs fat-free milk

NOTES:

Hummus: Look for one closer to 2 fat per serving, instead of the typical 5. I like Hope brand.

Tzatziki: Trader Joe's has an excellent store-bought option.

Feta: Trader Joe's sells fat-free.

1. **Make the salsa:** Chop all of your veggies nice and small. Remove any really juicy and seedy insides from the tomatoes. Toss with feta, mint, lemon juice, olive oil, and s&p.

2. **Make tzatziki:** If you're using the homemade version, grate cucumber, drain, and squeeze excess water out in a paper towel. Combine with Greek yogurt, garlic, fresh herbs, lemon juice, olive oil, and s&p. Add milk until desired consistency. Try to make this ahead of time so it can sit and marry for about 30 minutes.

3. Pan fry your carnitas in a hot pan for a couple of minutes. In another pan heat pitas, spraying each side with a mist of cooking spray and sprinkling with kosher salt.

4. Top each with about 1 Tbs of hummus, 50 g pork, 75 grams of greek salsa, butter lettuce, 1 Tbs tzatziki, and a generous squeeze of fresh lemon. SO GOOD.

P.S. I love to serve this meal when we have guests.

Feeding the family: Half of my family loves this! They eat theirs on the big, soft Papa Pitas and they're AMAZING. The little boys eat pork and pita separately, for now. Good enough for me!

Meal-prep thoughts: Meat, salsa, and tzatziki can all be made ahead. Salsa is best the first day, but it stays good for 3-4 days. It is much more watery and not as pretty but still delicious! It would be great packed as a salad with pita on the side. But that pita is really best hot off the pan.

NUTRITION

Serving size: 2 pitas
389 Cal/10.5F/40C/42P

Search MFP for:
"Lillie Eats and Tells Greek Pitas with Instant Pot Pork"

10-minute skinny cuban

. . . .

PREP: 25 MINUTES   TOTAL: 1 HOUR   SERVES: 1

For The Sandwich

1 bolillo roll or sliced French bread (70 g)

2 Tbs mojo "mayo" (recipe below)

1 Tbs yellow mustard

1 tsp honey mustard

1 slice lite Swiss)21 g)

About 4 oz Greek pork or salsa verde carnitas (120 g)

1.25 oz deli-sliced, honey-cured ham (35 g)

Thinly sliced pickles

Pepperoncinis or mild banana pepper rings (15 g)

Quick pickled onions (30 g)--pg 15

Big pinch of fresh cilantro

Arugula (optional)

For the Mojo "Mayo" just stir together:

1/2 cup light sour cream

2 cloves of garlic, minced (or frozen Dorot cubes)

1-2 Tbs fresh mint, chopped

1/2 Tbs fresh cilantro, chopped

Pinch of salt and pepper

. . . .

NUTRITION

. . . .

Serving size: 1 Sandwich
463 Cal/8F/51C/48.5P

Search MFP for:
"Lillie Eats and Tells 10 Minute Skinny Cuban Sandwich"

1. Pickle your onions--even if they'll only pickle while you prep everything else. Worth it.

2. Heat carnitas in a pan over medium-high heat with some garlic salt and an optional squeeze of orange juice. (If tracking, measure your portion before you pan-fry.)

3. Cut bolillo roll in half (if watching carbs, cut the bottom extra thin, then hollow out the top to reach desired weight in grams).

4. Spread with mojo "mayo" and mustards; top with cheese first, then pork, ham, pickles and/or pepperoncinis, pickled onions, cilantro, and arugula (if you love arugula and add greens to everything, like me!)

5. Top with other half of roll. Spray each side with cooking olive oil spray and cook in panini press, OR, heat a skillet over medium-high heat. Spray with cooking spray and add sandwich. Press with a heavy skillet on top until the bottom is golden brown. Spray top with olive spray and flip. Repeat. Enjoy!

. . . .

P.S. I buy Jarlsberg lite swiss cheese at the deli and have them slice it thin so I can get a larger surface area covered for 21 g.

I prefer to slice a whole pickle to get it thinner than pre- sliced pickles. (I'm actually not a huge fan of pickles and prefer only pepperoncinis, but they are a classic element so I didn't dare leave them out.)

Feeding the family: Feel free to do simple grilled ham and cheese for the littles. More pork for you!

Meal-prep thoughts: Paninis can be assembled a few hours ahead and then grilled just before eating. Make sure pork is somewhere in the middle, so it's less likely to make the bread soggy.

. . . .

lightened-up, bbq pulled-pork sandwich

WITH CILANTRO-LIME SLAW

PREP: 15 MINUTES   TOTAL: 15 MINUTES   SERVES: 8

For the Sandwich: (serves 1)
1 brioche bun
100 g instant pot bbq pulled pork
3 oz cilantro-lime slaw (recipe below) (80 g)
2.5 Tbs Stubb's barbecue sauce

For the Cilantro-Lime Slaw: (serves 6-8)
1 Tbs white wine vinegar
2 Tbs light-mayo
3 Tbs fresh squeezed lime juice
1/4 tsp salt
1/8 tsp pepper
1 tsp honey
1 12-oz bag of coleslaw mix
1/2 a red bell pepper, diced
1/4-1/2 cup green onion, chopped
1/4 cup apple, chopped (optional)
1 handful of cilantro

NOTES:

Brioche buns will be sold in the bakery of your grocery store. I find them at Walmart, Stater Brothers, and Sprouts. The macros should be about 25c/4f/5p. Feel free to use what you have and account for difference in macros, if tracking.

Bbq: I also like Hughes sugar-free bbq sauce.

Apples: If you choose to skip 'em, it makes a very small difference in macros for a serving.

1. Mix first six ingredients together for dressing (add up to 1/4 cup canola oil if you aren't watching your fat, I don't.)

2. Toss with remaining ingredients. It might seem dry at first, but it gets better as it sits for a little bit. If it still seems too dry, just add another squeeze of lime or dash of vinegar.

3. Spray the inside of the buns with cooking spray and pan-toast on a skillet. If you're feeding a crowd, you can also spray them and broil for a couple of minutes. Or, use your electric pancake griddle.

4. Immediately top with shredded pork, bbq sauce, and cilantro-lime apple slaw.

P.S. If the sandwiches will sit for any time, or if you're just worried about the juiciness, pan fry the pork for a bit to dry it out a little before assembling to avoid soggy buns. (But make this meal often, to avoid saggy buns. Ha!)

Feeding the family: All of my kids love this one! Hope yours do too. We love to serve with watermelon.

Meal-prep thoughts: Use pork and slaw in a bowl with rice or cauli rice for a great packed lunch. Or, bring buns to toast and build a sandwich if you have a toaster.

NUTRITION

Serving size: 1 sandwich as described
360 Cal/8F/45C/26P

Search MFP for:
"Lillie Eats and Tells Lightened Up Bbq Pulled Pork Sandwich with Cilantro Lime Slaw"

korean bbq pork tacos

PREP: 10 MINUTES   TOTAL: 40 MINUTES   SERVES: 1

3 Extra-thin Mission corn tortillas
4 oz bbq pulled pork (112 g)
Carrots, thinly sliced (30 g)
Cucumbers, thinly sliced (30 g)
Shredded cabbage
Radishes (optional)
Handful of cilantro
Pinch of fresh mint leaves
Green onions, chopped
Fresh jalapeño, diced
Avocado, sliced (20 g)
2 Tbs lite sour cream
Sriracha hot sauce

For the pickling liquid:
1/2 cup apple-cider vinegar
1 Tbs sugar
1.5 tsp kosher salt
1 cup water

NOTES:

Tortillas: I get the "extra-thin" tortillas at Walmart and Ralph's. They can be hard to find. They're 8 carbs per tortilla. All three come to 24c/1.5f/3p.

Cabbage: I love purple for color but any will do!

NUTRITION

Serving size: 3 tacos
383Cal/8.2F/42.2C/31.9P

Search MFP for:
"Lillie Eats and Tells Korean Bbq Pork Tacos"

1. **For the quick-pickled veggies:** Thinly slice your carrots, cucumbers, and radishes if using. (A mandolin is perfect for this if you have one! Cheap little gadget.) Place each veggie in separate bowls if you'd like to store them separately for later use. If it's just for this meal, feel free to combine.

2. Make one batch of the pickling liquid and pour some over each veggie and let it sit for 10-30 minutes.

3. **Make sriracha cream:** Just mix together lite sour cream with a splash of sriracha and a pinch of salt to taste. Thin it out with a little milk or even water if you want it to be runnier for easier drizzling and coverage.

4. **For the pork:** Heat a pan to medium-high heat, add some cooking spray and then the leftover pork. Season with a little garlic powder and a drizzle of sriracha. Cook for just a couple of minutes to reheat and crisp it up a little.

5. **Build your tacos:** Heat tortillas in a pan with some cooking spray, top with pork, about 30 grams of each pickled veggie (or as much as you want--these macros aren't going to do any damage!), a handful of fresh cilantro, some fresh mint if you love it like me, green onions, jalapenos, and about 30 grams total (or 2 tbs) of the sriracha cream. Enjoy!

P.S. For macro counters: When you reheat the meat in the pan, it shrinks. So, if you want to be accurate, you'll want to weigh your portion of 120 g before you throw it in the pan. (It will end up around 100 g after the pan-fry... but you'll still get all of the nutritional content from the 130 g.) If that's a pain, just estimate by taking only about 90-100 g of the crispy meat.

If you've got room for lots of protein, plan for more meat! I'd always love a larger portion of the pork.

Feeding the family: the kids can always just throw cheese and avocado on theirs!

Meal-prep thoughts: Package up the pork and toppings like a salad and bring tortillas on the side for heating and filling. Or, use a grain in place of tortillas to add to the bowl

bbq pulled-pork lavash quesadilla

PREP: 5 MINUTES   TOTAL: 10 MINUTES   SERVES: 1

1 Joseph's lavash wrap
4 oz bbq pulled-pork (112 g)
1 wedge Laughing Cow Spicy Pepper Jack cheese
1/2 oz lite shredded three-cheese blend(14 g)
Apples, thinly sliced (30 g)
Red onion, thinly sliced (25 g)
1 Tbs Stubb's bbq sauce
Handful of cilantro
1 Tbs Bolthouse Classic Ranch for dipping

NOTES:

Wrap: For this recipe, I use the Joseph's lavash wrap. I get mine at Walmart and they're a must if you have them at yours. If not, they're also on Amazon. I also REALLY love the Cut Da Carb wraps, which are only available online.

Cheese: I like the lite three-cheese blend from Trader Joe's and use it in this recipe.

NUTRITION

Serving size: 1 whole quesadilla with 1 Tbs ranch
435 Cal/12.4F/35.6C/45.4P

Search MFP for:
"Lillie Eats and Tells Macro Friendly Bbq Pulled Pork Lavash Quesadilla"

1. Heat lavash wrap in a pan.

2. Spread half of the wrap's long side with the Laughing Cow, then top with pork, bbq sauce, apple, red onion, plenty of cilantro, and shredded cheese.

3. Fold other half over, forming a rectangular quesadilla and spray with olive oil mist and sprinkle with kosher salt.

4. Flip and do the same with the other side.
Serve with greens drizzled with Bolthouse Ranch and extra Ranch for dipping.

P.S. You could also fold this "crunch-wrap" style if you'd like it more contained! There's a video on my Instagram stories for a visual.

Feeding the family: Mine is on a lavash and theirs are on basic flour tortillas but we all eat together!

Meal-prep thoughts: Reheats great in a pan or toaster oven.

bbq pulled-pork on protein waffles

WITH CILANTRO-LIME SLAW

PREP: 5 MINUTES   **TOTAL:** 10 MINUTES   **SERVES:** 1

For the bbq pulled-pork on waffle (serves 1):
1 protein waffle (recipe below)
2 oz bbq pulled-pork (56 g)
1/3 cup cilantro-lime slaw (50 g)-- pg 33
1 Tbs Hughes sugar-free bbq sauce (15 g)

Protein Waffles (makes 3):
1/2 cup Kodiak Cakes® pancake mix (53 g)
1/4 cup pumpkin (or unsweetened applesauce) (60 g)
1 whole egg
1 scoop PEScience® Snickerdoodle protein powder
1/3 cup Fairlife fat-free milk (90 g)
1/2 tsp vanilla
Dash of cinnamon

NOTES:

Protein powder: Feel free to use your favorite vanilla protein powder or other complimentary
flavor. I love this one in waffles.

Milk: Unsweetened Califia Farms vanilla almond
milk is great too! It'll add a little fat and a few less
carbs. Doesn't change macros much.

NUTRITION

Serving size: 1 topped waffle as described
220 Cal/4F/18C/28P

Search MFP for:
"Lillie Eats and Tells Bbq Pulled Pork on Protein
Waffles"

1. Whisk together all waffle ingredients until smooth.

2. Spray waffle iron with non-stick spray (I use a small-hole
thin waffle iron, not belgian.) And cook 1/3 of the batter at a
time. It should make three waffles.

3. Top hot waffle with 55 g bbq pulled-pork, 50 g cilantro-lime slaw, and a drizzle of bbq sauce (1 tbs).

4. For a few more macros, top with 10-20 g avocado. I also
love a drizzle of sugar-free syrup, or of course pure maple
syrup or honey if you've got a few carbs to spare!

P.S. If you want to be perfectly precise, you can weigh your
batter (subtracting the bowl) to know how much 1/3 will be.
This should make three waffles in your average small-hole
waffle iron. The macros listed are for ONE waffle.

I usually eat TWO topped waffles, but figured it would be easier
to give you the option to log just ONE and go from there!
Freeze the third for a quick breakfast.

Meal-prep thoughts: The waffles can be made ahead and
frozen. Toast right before dinner (or for a quick breakfast). They
might need a quick defrost or thaw to make sure the middle
toasts all the way through.

Feeding the family: I usually make the protein waffles for
myself, but, for my family, I either whip up a batch of normal
waffles OR cook up the Trader Joe's Cornbread mix as waffles.
(AMAZING.)

bbq pulled-pork and peach grilled cheese

PREP: 5 MINUTES   TOTAL: 10 MINUTES   SERVES: 1

Two pieces of thinly sliced French bread or roll (40 g)

115 g instant pot bbq pork

1 slice lite havarti cheese (28 g)

½ slice lite swiss cheese (10 g)

Caramelized onion (15 g)

Thinly sliced peaches (25 g)

1 Tbs Stubb's bbq sauce

NOTES:

Bread: I like to use my big "bolillo" or "pane" rolls from my grocery store bakery. They are light and airy and allow for larger surface area with less weight which means fewer carbs! I slice the long sandwich roll into 3-4 horizontal thin slices, and use two of the slices (equaling 40 g.)

Cheese: I get the lite Havarti at Trader Joe's. I just use the Swiss to bulk up the cheese because it's lower fat than the Havarti--feel free to do all Havarti! I get my lite Jarlsberg Swiss at the deli counter so I can get it sliced extra thin and have it cover more area for the same weight. It's sold presliced at Costco and most stores.

Caramelized onion: Sauté thinly sliced onion in cooking spray and a pinch of kosher salt over medium-low heat for 20-30 minutes while you prep dinner. You want them super soft and sweet.

If peaches are out of season: Apples would be good, too. Or fig butter from Trader Joe's.

Bbq sauce: Sugar-free Hughes from Walmart is another option with lower carbs.

1. Use two slices from the middle of the roll, or two extra-thin slices of your bread equaling 40 g.

2. Top bottom slice with cheese, pork, caramelized onion, peaches, and bbq sauce. Top with other piece of bread.

3. Spray both sides of sandwich with cooking spray and brown in a pan on medium-high heat until toasted and cheese is melty.

P.S. Sometimes I like to open it up and add slaw if I have it leftover from pulled pork sandwiches!

Bread-tracking tip: If you are a macro-counter and not sure how to track unlabeled bread, search, for example, "bolillo roll g" (or whatever the name of your roll is plus the letter "g" for grams) in MFP to find an option in grams. Look for one you can trust from Walmart or some chain. It should be around 32 carbs for 65 g of bread. Finding "1 bolillo" could vary so much. It's all about the weight for accuracy! Now you can log as much as you eat.

Feeding the family: My family loves these! For picky eaters, just make some simple grilled cheese. Serve with a simple salad.

Meal-prep thoughts: You could assemble it and grill later, but, if so, make sure to crisp up your meat in a pan beforehand to dry it out so it doesn't soak your bread.

NUTRITION

Serving size: 1 sandwich
384 Cal/8.6F/32.6C/40P

Search MFP for:
"Lillie Eats and Tells Bbq Pulled Pork and Peach Grilled Cheese"

bbq pork and rice skillet

PREP: 15 MINUTES   TOTAL: 20 MINUTES   SERVES: 3-4

1/2 onion, diced (180 g)
1/2 bell pepper, diced (90 g)
5-6 cups frozen or fresh cauliflower rice (600 g)
1 Laughing Cow Pepper Jack Cheese wedge
1 clove of garlic, minced (or frozen cube)
1/4 cup fresh cilantro, chopped
2 cups precooked brown rice (280 g)
Salt and pepper
About 14 oz instant pot bbq pulled-pork (400 g)
1.5 oz (full fat) sharp white cheddar cheese (40 g)

Additional optional toppings
Avocado
Sweet corn
Tomatoes
Favorite bbq sauce
Lightened up cilantro-lime ranch-- pg 14

NOTES:

Rice: We love the frozen pouches of brown rice or jasmine, if you prefer, from Trader Joe's.

Laughing Cow: You could also use some light cream cheese, Greek yogurt cream cheese, or maybe even just a few tablespoons of Greek yogurt (haven't tried it). Macros won't change much-- it's a small portion. Use about 1 oz.

Cheese: I did the math to see if it was worth subbing in Trader Joe's lite three-cheese blend and it'll save you 2 g of fat per serving. So I say no! Ha. Up to you. But, sometimes I just really want to TASTE a good strong cheese.

NUTRITION

Serving size: 350 g before additional toppings
351 Cal/7.2F/40C/32.4P

Search MFP for:
"Lillie Eats and Tells Bbq Pork and Rice Skillet"

1. Heat a small cast-iron skillet or oven-safe pan over medium-high heat. Spray with cooking spray.

2. Add diced onion and bell pepper, season with salt and pepper. Sauté for a few minutes.

3. Add cauliflower rice and cook for another 5 minutes until cauliflower is tender. Add Laughing Cow cheese wedge and garlic, and sauté for another minute until the cheese is melted and everything is combined.

4. Add cilantro, pre-cooked brown rice, and pulled pork to the skillet and combine. If the pan is sized right, smooth out mixture and top with sharp cheddar. If not, transfer to an oven-safe dish (8x8 or slightly smaller) and top with cheese.

5. Put skillet (or dish) in the broiler for 5 minutes or until cheese is bubbly. Drizzle with (optional) bbq sauce, cilantro-lime-ranch, and whatever your heart desires. (I hope that includes avocado.) Pair this with a simple green salad!

P.S. I actually really like the sugar-free Hughes bbq sauce. If you prefer not to use artificial sweeteners, Stubb's is a good naturally lower carb option. My family loves a yummy homemade sauce or your good old Sweet Baby Rays®.

Feeding the family: Double this recipe if you think they'll like it. Mine does! And sometimes I keep some extra brown rice out to bulk up their bowls. They top generously with avocado etc.

Meal-prep thoughts: A perfect one to pack and enjoy as leftovers! Just heat and eat.

GRILLED CHICKEN

Don't feel limited by which chicken marinade will work in which recipe. The macros are all so similar and you'll be suprised at how versatile they all are. Just use what you have!

THE PROTEIN

APPLE-CIDER DIJON GRILLED CHICKEN 47

GREEK-MARINATED GRILLED CHICKEN SKEWERS 48

MOROCCAN-MARINATED CHICKEN SKEWERS 51

THE MEALS

CHICKEN "PESTO" PANINI 52

SKINNY CHICKEN DIVAN 54

LAVASH BBQ CHICKEN AND PEAR PIZZA 57

MEDITERRANEAN ARUGULA AND GRAIN BOWL 58

QUICK THAI CHICKEN SALAD 61

CREAMY MUSHROOM CAULIFLOWER RISOTTO 62

VEGGIE, FETA, AND CHICKEN LAVASH PIZZA 65

GRILLED CHICKEN AND VEGGIE RAINBOW BOWL 66

PEACH AND BACON FLATBREADS 69

ROASTED TOMATO-BASIL CHICKEN SANDWICH 70

MEDITERRANEAN CHICKEN FLATBREADS 73

THAI CAULIFLOWER FRIED RICE 74

apple-cider dijon grilled chicken

PREP: 20 MINUTES   TOTAL: 6 MINUTES   SERVES: 10–12

6 lbs chicken tenderloins
1/3 cup apple-cider vinegar
3-4 Tbs (I use 4) grainy dijon mustard
1 tsp honey (7 g)
12-16 cloves of garlic, minced (frozen cubes)
1.5-2 Tbs kosher salt
1/2 Tbs pepper

NOTES:

I use one whole bag of Costco frozen chicken tenderloins. I really prefer tenderloins to breasts. They cook up so fast and are so much more tender for me with no texture issues.

You can sub any white balsamic or champagne vinegar for apple cider vinegar.

Sometimes I like to add fresh herbs if I have them on hand (or extra honey or fresh citrus). This is our basic weekly, go-in-anything chicken.

NUTRITION

Serving size: 100 g grilled chicken
130 Cal/1.3F/0C/29.9P

Search MFP for:
"Lillie Eats and Tells Weekly Bulk Apple Cider Dijon Grilled Chicken"

1. Thaw tenderloins and trim fat and weird strings and tendony stuff (ew!). Pat dry and place in large Ziplock.

2. Whisk all marinade ingredients together and pour over chicken. Close bag and work the marinade so it spreads around. Let marinate anywhere from an hour to overnight. Longer marinade = more flavor, of course!

3. Preheat grill to medium high (I usually err on the hotter side).

4. Spray grill with cooking spray (carefully since it will make the flame go wild for a second).

5. Sprinkle a little more kosher salt over chicken and grill for 2-3 minutes per side. Make sure and get nice, dark marks on the first side (you can always pull off early on the flip side if needed). At least that way you know you'll guarantee some nice color.

P.S. Let me explain the high protein: when chicken is grilled, it loses so much water and reduces a lot in weight. The nutritional content becomes much more condensed. So you'll notice when you're eating chicken from the instant pot, or even baked, the same 113 g portion will be lower in protein and overall macros. That's because you're getting more water in that weight as well.

This chicken freezes great! Just thaw and chop for salads or BARELY warm for sandwiches, etc. according to recipes.

greek-marinated grilled chicken skewers

WITH GARLIC, LEMON, AND HERBS

PREP: 30 MINUTES   TOTAL: 1–2 HOURS MINUTES   SERVES: 6

2-2.5 lbs of chicken breasts
1/4 cup fresh oregano, finely chopped
1/4 cup fresh parsley, finely chopped
7 cloves of garlic, minced (or frozen cubes)
Juice from 1-2 lemons (about 6 Tbs)
1 Tbs olive oil
1/2 tsp red chili flakes
1 tsp cumin
1.5 tsp kosher salt
1/2 tsp fresh ground pepper

NOTES:

Oil: If you don't count your macros and the added fat is not a concern to you, add 1/4-/1/2 cup olive oil! And if you do, you can marinate for longer.

If you track macros and you do a little more or less chicken than I did, it's FINE. This variance won't affect the macros much since your portion will be in grams and not, for example 1/8th of the recipe. It will only slightly affect the distribution of the marinade, which is so low cal anyway. And if you have marinade left in the bag, it's FINE. For the same reason.

NUTRITION

Serving size: 100 g grilled chicken
163 Cal/3.4F/2.1C/29.4P

Search MFP for:
"Lillie Eats and Tells Greek Marinated Chicken Skewers"

1. Chop chicken into 1 1/2 inch pieces and place in a large Ziplock. (This is one of the only recipes I prefer to use huge fresh chicken breasts rather than chicken tenderloins. They're nice for chopping good chunks. But tenderloins work, too.)

2. Whisk together all marinade ingredients, pour over the chicken, and seal the bag. Move it all around to make sure it's nice and covered. Marinate up to two hours. With so much acid and so little fat, you don't want this to marinate all night or it can make the chicken tough.

3. Use metal skewers OR soak wooden skewers in water for thirty minutes to help avoid burning. Then thread your chicken, making sure to leave some ends to grab! (You can also cover the ends in foil to protect them from burning, if needed.)

4. Spray the skewered chicken with a mist of cooking spray on each side, sprinkle with a pinch of kosher salt, and grill on a preheated, oiled* grill or grill pan over medium-high heat for 4-5 minutes per side, until you have nice color and it's cooked through.

5. Serve with a fresh squeeze of lemon and homemade tzatziki--in a Greek salad, pita or grain bowl. The possibilities are endless!

P.S. I always spray the grill with cooking spray, but be careful! The flame will climb when you do.

Feel free to use tenderloins and skip the skewers! We just like them for change some times.

moroccan-marinated chicken skewers

WITH OIL-FREE BASIL PARSLEY PESTO

PREP: 30 MINUTES   TOTAL: 2 HOURS   SERVES: 12–14

4 lbs chicken breasts or tenderloins
  cut into 1.5-inch chunks
2/3 cup fat-free Greek yogurt
2 Tbs olive oil
10 cloves of garlic, minced (or frozen cubes)
3 Tbs rice wine vinegar (or lemon juice)
2-3 Tbs cilantro, chopped
1 Tbs ginger paste (or minced fresh ginger)
1.5 Tbs cumin
1 Tbs paprika
2 tsp kosher salt
1 tsp black pepper

I love to serve this with this pesto below:

Oil-Free Basil Parsley Pesto
2 cups fresh herbs (I used half basil, half parsley)
3 Tbs non-fat Greek yogurt
3 Tbs orange-flavored vinegar (Trader Joe's)
1.5 Tbs toasted pine nuts (20 g)
1 clove of garlic, minced (or frozen cube)
Sprinkle of salt, pepper + pinch of red pepper flakes

NOTES:

Vinegar: I use the orange muskat vinegar from Trader Joe's but any white balsamic vinegar will work. I just love the sweet hint that a fruity vinegar adds.

Toasted pine nuts: I find these for the best price at Trader Joe's.

NUTRITION

Serving size: 100 g grilled chicken
155 Cal/3F/1.5C/27.5P/9.8/Fiber 0
Serving size: 30 g pesto
50 Cal/2.9F/4.9C/2.1P

Search MFP for:
"Lillie Eats and Tells Moroccan Chicken Skewers" & "Lillie Eats and Tells Oil-Free Basil Parsley Pesto"

1. Combine all marinade ingredients in a bowl large enough to add the chicken to. Once it's mixed, add the chunks of chicken and toss to coat. Cover or transfer to a large Ziploc bag and marinate for 30 minutes to overnight.

2. Make pesto by pulsing all ingredients in a small food processor or blender until it's your desired consistnency.

3. Use metal skewers, OR soak wooden skewers in water for 30 minutes to help avoid burning. Then thread your chicken, making sure to leave some ends to grab! (You can also cover the ends in foil to protect them from burning, if needed).

4. Spray the skewered chicken with a mist of cooking spray on each side, sprinkle with a fresh pinch of kosher salt, and grill on a preheated, oiled* grill or grill pan (or a sauté pan will work!) over medium-high heat for about 5 minutes per side (or until you have nice color and the chicken is cooked through).

P.S. I always spray the grill with cooking spray, but be careful! The flame will climb when you do.

Taking the extra time to skewer chicken is not always worth it to me when I could just marinate tenderloins and throw those on the grill without being elbow-deep in it. BUT, I LOVE to do skewers if we're having people over or I'm bringing dinner to a friend, since it has such better presentation. It's also my go-to if fresh chicken breasts are on sale at my grocery store. I don't love how an entire chicken breast grills--the texture can be too bouncy or tough for me--so, if I'm working with whole breasts, I like to chop them to sauté for fajitas or stir-fries OR skewer them. Plus you get so many more grilled crispy, salty edges. YUM.

chicken *"pesto"* panini

PREP: 5 MINUTES   TOTAL: 10 MINUTES   SERVES: 1

2 slices of thinly siced French or Italian bread (50 g)

3.5 oz grilled chicken (100 g)

1 Tbs (15 g) light basil garlic aioli-- pg 12

1.5 slices (32 g) lite Havarti cheese

Sliced roma tomatoes

A handful of arugula

NOTES:

Bread: I like the double pack of fresh loaves from Costco. They're uncut, so I can try and cut the slices as thinly as possible for maximum sandwich with MINI-MUM carb count. My goal is to get the slices to weigh close to 50 grams in total in order for these macros to be accurate.

Cheese: Mozzarella or provolone would also be great.

NUTRITION

Serving size: 1 panini as described
365 Cal/9F/26C/43P

Search MFP for:
"Lillie Eats and Tells Chicken Pesto Panini"

1. Take two very thin slices of bread, totaling around 50 g. Top the bottom slice with 1 tbs of basil garlic aioli and one slice of cheese.

2. Arrange leftover tenderloins butterflied at an angle to fit just right.

3. Top with sliced tomato, arugula, and extra half slice of cheese, then second piece of bread.

4. Spray the outside of the sandwich with cooking spray and cook over medium-hight heat until the cheese is melty and the bread is toasty.

P.S. I know this isn't pesto--but I keep trying to make a yummy macro-friendly pesto, and it's hard! Pesto really wants to be swimming with olive oil and nuts. With this guilt-free creamy base, you get all the flavor and keep your fats super low.

Takes 10 minutes to throw together with leftover grilled chicken. It's easy enough for lunch but legit enough for dinner paired with a simple salad. And/or maybe a second panini. SO GOOD.

Feeding the family: Pull out your pancake griddle for lots of paninis (or grilled cheese for the extra picky ones) at once.

Meal-prep thoughts: You could build ahead of time, keeping tomatoes out. Then right before dinner, add tomatoes and cook it up.

skinny chicken divan

PREP: 20 MINUTES   TOTAL: 55 MINUTES   SERVES: 6–8

For the Cauliflower Cream Sauce (if you like things extra saucy, double this recipe)

10 oz cauliflower (1/2 head or bagged florets)

1 cup chicken stock

1/2 Tbs butter

4 cloves of garlic, minced (I use frozen dorot cubes)

1/2 tsp salt

1/4 tsp pepper

1/4 cup fat-free milk

(These last two ingredients I only add when the sauce is specifically for this divan.)

1 tsp curry powder

1 Tbs fresh lemon juice

For the Chicken Divan

4 cups chopped **grilled chicken** (530 g dijon bulk)

20 oz broccoli florets, steamed according to package

2 oz full-fat sharp sheddar

2 cups white bread, chopped into big crumbs (90 g)

Cauliflower cream sauce (it should be about 6-700 g)

. . . .

NUTRITION

. . . .

Serving size: 400 g
313 Cal/8F/18C/44.5P

Search MFP for:
"Lillie Eats and Tells Skinny Chicken Divan"

Make the Cauliflower Cream Sauce

1. Cook cauliflower by preferred method. You can boil in chicken stock or simply microwave a bag until soft.

2. While the cauliflower cooks, sauté the garlic and butter in a large nonstick skillet over LOW heat. Cook for several minutes until the garlic is soft and fragrant but not brown. You don't want it bitter. Remove from heat and set aside.

3. Add cauliflower, 1 cup of chicken stock, the sautéed garlic/butter, salt, pepper, curry, lemon and milk. Blend or puree for a few minutes until the sauce is very smooth. You can add more broth or milk depending on how thick you want the sauce.

Make the Divan

1. Preheat oven to 350 and spray 9x13 with nonstick cooking spray.

2. Combine cooked broccoli (salt to taste), chopped cooked chicken and sauce (in a large bowl so everything gets coated. If you've doubled the sauce, feel free to add a little more, you can estimate how much extra you'll get and log it serately from MFP (it has its own listing), or even add some to your individual servings.

3. Transfer mixture to your 9x13, sprinkle with cheese and top with bread crumbs. Spray the top of the bread crumbs with a mist of cooking spray, and sprinkle with kosher salt.

4. Bake for 35 minutes uncovered until bread crumbs are golden brown.

NOTES:

Cheese: I love to use a specialty onion and chive cheese from Trader Joe's, or an extra sharp white, but any cheddar is great. You could double the cheese and only add a few more grams of fat to each portion, if a portion is about 1/6th of a 9x13. If you've got room, that would be all the yummier! Of course you could use low-fat cheese if you like that, too. I wanted something with flavor!

Bread Crumbs: I highly recommend chopping up your own bread for nice big bread crumbs rather than store-bought bread crumbs. It creates such better volume and texture.

Sauce: I would recommend doubling the sauce if you like things saucier or want additional for serving over a grain. You could wait to add the curry and lemon until after you separate it in half, then you can decide if you want to add it to the other half to use for this meal, or save the leftover sauce for a pasta, or spaghetti squash dinner later in the week. I've blended in parmesan, basil, marinara... the possibilities are endless!

For logging purposes: If you log the Chicken Divan directly from MFP the macros account for the recipe as is; but, there is another option for just "Lillie Eats and Tells Cauliflower Cream Sauce." So you can log your portion of Divan from MFP and then any additional sauce you may use.

Feeding the Family: My kids love this and eat it over pasta or potatoes. I like mine over cauliflower rice, spaghetti squash, or, just plain.

Meal-prep thoughts: I haven't tried freezing, but I think it would work great to freeze and bake later! You can definitely assemble it a couple of days ahead and store in your fridge to bake later in the week. The cauliflower cream sauce alone DOES freeze well, and I've had readers say they freeze it as ice cubes to use later.

Once baked, leftovers can be broiled or baked until hot and top is toasty again. Works great. You might want to add some extra sauce on your leftovers as it can get soaked up as it sits.

lavash bbq chicken and pear pizza

PREP: 10 MINUTES   TOTAL: 15 MINUTES   SERVES: 1

1 Joseph's lavash wrap
3 Tbs of low-fat ricotta (50 g) mixed with
  half a cube of frozen garlic (or half a clove, minced)
1-2 tsp reduced fat blue cheese (6 g)
1 Tbs caramelized onion (15 g)
Small handful of pear (or apple), thinly sliced (30 g)
1/3 cup grilled chicken (45 g)
Red onion, thinly sliced
1 Tbs Hughes sugar-free bbq sauce (15 g)
Arugula

NOTES:

Wraps: The Joseph's lavash bread can be found on Amazon and at many Walmarts. Cut Da Carb wraps are another amazing option, though they are available only online. For pizzas, I prefer Lavash because they're sturdier than the Cut Da Carb and still have pretty amazing macros. Feel free to use your favorite wrap and adjust your macros.

Reduced- fat blue cheese: I find reduced-fat blue cheese at Stater Brothers by the brand "Treasure Cave." If you can't find it, I would just spend the fat on a slightly smaller amount of real blue cheese--you just can't substitute that flavor! And a little goes a long way.

I find Hughes sugar-free at Walmart. Stubb's is another good option.

NUTRITION

Serving size: 1 pizza
308 Cal/8F/34C/28P

Search MFP for:
"Lillie Eats and Tells Bbq Chicken and Pear Pizza"

1. To caramelize onions, spray with cooking spray and sprinkle with kosher salt. Cook on medium-low for 20-30 min till soft. You can do this ahead of time and keep in your fridge for all of your burgers, sandwiches, and pizzas!

2. Spray lavash with olive oil spray and sprinkle with kosher salt. Pre-bake at 450 for 3-5 minutes until lavash is golden and slightly crispy.

3. Stir together ricotta and garlic and spread on par-baked lavash, then top with reduced-fat blue cheese, caramelized onion, pear, chicken, and red onion.

4. Bake for another 3-5 minutes until the edges are brown, being careful not to burn.

5. Cut in pizza wedges and drizzle with 15 g bbq sauce and sprinkle with fresh cilantro. Pile on arugula and a drizzle of Bolthouse ranch if you're into that kind of thing.

P.S. If you've got fat to spare, a layer of mozzarella would be great, or some avocado as an additional topping.

If you track macros and want to track your own portoins of this meal: for the onions, I just log 30 g raw onion and USE 15 g of caramelized onion since it shrinks by half when you cook. Make plenty and save for burgers/pizzas/paninis etc!

Feeding the family: When we have a family pizza night, I use the big soft Papa Pita breads for my family, and we all do the toppings we like--usually, pepperoni and red sauce for the boys, pesto and chicken for girls, and all the chopped veggies for me. (I love to store some chopped veggies in Ziplocs to repeat this pizza for the next couple of days.)

mediterranean arugula and grain bowl

PREP: 10 MINUTES   TOTAL: 15 MINUTES   SERVES: 1

1/2 cup cooked brown rice (70 g)

A heaping handful of arugula (75 g)

3.5 oz grilled Greek chicken (100 g)

2/3 cup cucumber salsa (100 g)--pg 29

2 Tbs tzatziki (30 g)--pg 29

2.5 Tbs hummus (40 g)

Pickled red onion (25 g)--pg 15

Pickled cabbage (25 g)*

1/2 oz of fat-free feta (14 g)

Extra mint

Squeeze of lemon

NOTES:

Rice: We love the frozen brown rice from Trader Joe's.

Chicken: Of course the Greek chicken makes the most sense, but, really, any leftover grilled chicken or shredded pork is delicious in this!

The recipe for cucumber salsa and tzatiziki is on the Greek pita recipe, pg 29. The cucumber salsa is a MUST! But Trader Joe's has a great Tzatziki that I use when I'm out of time.

Hummus: I love Hope® brand jalapeno cilantro-- it's only 2.5 g of fat for 2 Tbs, so if you want the macros to match, try and find one similar! I get Hope brand at Walmart.

***Pickled cabbage:** Just pour some of your pickling liquid from the onion recipe over sliced purple cabbage as well, (keeping them divided) for about 30 minutes to an hour. Store in fridge (in liquid) for up to a week.

1. Toss brown rice and arugula in a large bowl.

2. Top with chopped grilled Greek chicken, cucumber salsa, tzatziki, hummus, pickled onion and cabbage. Add feta, mint, and a squeeze of lemon and close your eyes and dream that you're at Cava.

P.S. This is the perfect meal to make with your Greek leftovers. I love to make a big batch of the chicken, or Greek pork, cucumber salsa, and tzatziki... and use it for pitas one night, and a bowl a night or two later. I've usually got pickled onions already in my fridge, so it's easy to pour some of the liquid over my cabbage and let it sit while I prep anything else.

This bowl is inpsired by one of my all-time casual quick restaurants, Cava. It's like the Chipotle of Mediterranean food, and it's HEAVENLY. (AND, they have their nutrition facts online--so you know I'm all over that!)

Feeding the family: My recipe is to give you guidance on a good portion size, but, of course, this is a great meal to just have everything out for build-your-own bowls or salads. Pickier kids can just eat rice and chicken. I'll often chop some fruit for them to have on the side.

Meal-prep thoughts: This is a great one for packaging up as everything can be eaten cool or room temp.

NUTRITION

Serving size: This bowl as described
478 Cal/13F/46C/47P

Search MFP for:
"Lillie Eats and Tells Copy Cat Cava Mediterranean Grain Bowl"

quick thai chicken salad

PREP: 10 MINUTES   TOTAL: 10 MINUTES   SERVES: 1

2-3 cups butter lettuce, chopped (130 g)
Handful of cucumber, chopped (30 g)
Handful of shredded carrots (30 g)
Handful of bell pepper, chopped small (30 g)
Handful of shredded cabbage (30 g)
2 Tbs green onion, chopped
1/4 cup or big pinch of cilantro, chopped
1/4 cup or big pinch of fresh mint (makes it!)
A few slices of avocado (15 g)
1/4 cup edamame (35 g)
Small handful of mango, chopped (25 g)
Small handful of radishes, sliced thin or chopped (15 g)
3.5 oz chopped grilled chicken (100 g)
1 Tbs Trader Joe's Spicy Peanut Vinaigrette (15 g)
2 Tbs Newmans Own Sesame Ginger Dressing (30 g)

NOTES:

Dressings: You can use just one dressing--I just love the flavor of the Trader Joe's but I like to make the macros stretch farther by combining it with Newman's own which is lighter. Both are delicious.

Optional add-ins: Trader Joe's Thai Cashews or toasted almonds, peanuts, rice noodles, linguini, or even zoodles, or shrimp.

NUTRITION

Serving size: This bowl as described
302 Cal/10F/30C/28P

Search MFP for:
"Lillie Eats and Tells Quick Thai Chicken Salad"

1. Just toss everything together! Always add a good sprinkling of kosher salt and cracked pepper. I like to especially make sure that my avocado and edamame get salted.

P.S.

Macro Tip: If you build this in your MFP diary yourself (or any salad) make sure and "save as meal" in My Fitness Pal after you log the whole thing once. This is especially helpful with salads or things with a bunch of ingredients. Now, you can add your "Thai Chicken Salad" to lunch tomorrow and build your big salad on your scale, zeroing out after each addition and adding the same amount as the day before, so you never have to touch your phone or scribble on some note pad. I hated that phase in the beginning of tracking!

Feeding the family: I'll either: toss my own and then throw whatever amounts in a huge bowl for them.

OR, make it a salad bar kind of thing where everyone builds their own. (We do this ALOT);

OR, multiply this whole thing by 4, weigh the final salad (minus the bowl), and calculate your fourth. Usually the rest of myfamily will bulk theirs up with more avocado and nuts and maybe noodles for the kids, so they won't want as much as me!

Meal-prep thoughts: I love to chop a bunch of these ingredients and store them in small baggies tucked into one big tupperware in the fridge. That way I can pull it out and toss a salad multiple times that week. I always chop the mango and avocado fresh. Other veggies last a few days diced. Great to pack for lunch with dressings on the side.

creamy mushroom-cauliflower risotto

WITH GRILLED CHICKEN

PREP: 20 MINUTES   TOTAL: 35 MINUTES RISOTTO SERVES: 2–3

In the blender (then added to pan):
10-oz bag of cauliflower steamed
1 oz shaved parmesan (28 g)
1/4 cup non-fat Greek yogurt (60 g)

In the pan:
8 oz mushrooms, sliced
1 cup white onion, diced (100 g)
14 oz riced cauliflower
1 clove of garlic, minced (or frozen cube)
1/2 tsp salt
1-2 Tbs fresh rosemary, minced

In the bowl:
About 1 cup of finished risotto (250 g)
3.5 oz grilled chicken, chopped (100 g)
Handful of cherry tomatoes (50 g)
Handful of arugula, tossed in lemon juice

NOTES:

Cauliflower: If it's annoying to buy two kinds of cauliflower, just use 24 oz of riced cauliflower and steam 10 oz of it. I just love the ease of the steamable bag of florets.

1. Blend steamed cauliflower (I just throw the bag in the microwave for 4 minutes) with Greek yogurt and parmesan till smooth and creamy. Set aside.

2. Heat a heavy-bottom pan over medium-high heat, spray with cooking spray, and add mushrooms and onions. Sprinkle with half the salt (1/4 tsp) and sauté for 3-5 minutes (or until soft.) Add riced cauliflower and continue to cook for about five minutes (or until cauliflower is tender, browned a little, and there's no excess liquid.) If using frozen cauliflower rice, you might need to use a lid and drain any excess water mid-cook. Stir in the frozen cube of garlic, rosemary, and another 1/4 tsp salt. Cook for one more minute. **TURN OFF HEAT.**

3. Pour blended cauliflower mixture into the pan and combine everything! Push risotto to one side of pan, add chopped, grilled chicken in the other half, and cover for just a minute. You don't want your chicken to taste reheated. JUST not cold. (You can stir it in if you're not worried about tracking your portion.) Otherwise:

4. Add 250 g risotto to a bowl and top with 100 g chopped grilled chicken, a little arugula, and cherry tomatoes if you like. Finish with fresh parmesan and fresh herbs!

P.S. This is surprisingly high in protein before you even top with chicken because of the Greek yogurt, parmesan, and mushrooms. Did you know mushrooms have as much protein as carbs? I'll include an MFP listing for the risotto by itself, so it's easy to log that and your own portion of chicken.

Feeding the family: If you don't think your kids will touch the risotto, heat a bag of frozen brown rice from Trader Joe's, or make some simple buttered pasta. We do lots of easy starch swaps for kids over here.

Meal-prep thoughts: Risotto freezes great for later! Just thaw and reheat in oven until warm.

NUTRITION

Serving size: 1 Bowl as described
305 Cal/4.3F/23C/44P
But for 250 g risotto alone:
158 cal/2.6F/19.5C/13.6P

Search MFP for:
"Lillie Eats and Tells Creamy mushroom cauliflower
risotto" and then log your own chicken and tomatoes! That seems easier for this one.

veggie, feta and chicken lavash pizza

PREP: 10 MINUTES   TOTAL: 15-20 MINUTES   SERVES: 1

1 Joseph's lavash bread
1-2 tsp garlic (thawed frozen Dorot cube)
1/4 cup jarred marinara
2 oz (almost) of grilled chicken, chopped (50 g)
1.5 Tbs fat-free feta (20 g)
Red onion, thinly sliced (20 g)
1 oz mushrooms, chopped small
Handful of cherry tomatoes, halved (40 g)
1 oz roasted red peppers (28 g)
1/2 oz pepperoncinis (jarred banana peppers) (14 g)
Small handful of peaches, thinly sliced (20 g)
Handful of arugula
A drizzle of balsamic glaze (3 g)

NOTES:

Marinara: Organic Victoria from Costco is my current fave, Trader Joe's Rustico also has great macros (but 1/4 cup of any brand won't kill your macros.)

Peaches: Apples, figs, pears, or the more classic pineapple would also be good if you're into a sweet kick on your pizza like me!

Balsamic Glaze: I get mine at Trader Joe's but have also picked up some yummy ones at Homegoods.

NUTRITION

Serving size: 1 whole pizza
334 Cal/5.3F/33C34.8P

Search MFP for:
"Lillie Eats and Tells Veggie Feta and Chicken Lavash Pizza"

1. Preheat oven to 450. Lay out your lavash on a cookie sheet or pizza pan if you have one, and spread with 1-2 tsp of minced garlic. (See notes if you like a crispier crust!)

2. Spread with red sauce. Then, top with chicken, feta, and veggies. Finish with a good sprinkle of kosher salt, and a mist of olive oil spray. Bake for 5-8 minutes (or until the edges are brown and crispy!)

3. Transfer to a large cutting board and cut in pizza wedges (or rectangles, if you prefer.) Top with a big handful of arugula, another sprinkle of kosher salt, and a drizzle of balsamic glaze. Eat off the cutting board for full effect!

P.S. The middle does stay soft, which doesn't bother me. But, if you want it crispier all the way through, you could bake the lavash for a few minutes first before you top it. Then bake again.

Feeding the family: Just like the bbq pizza, I make this on a family pizza night. We pull out the lavash or Joseph's pitas for me, and the Papa Pitas for the family. Everyone can build their own pizza, and they each bake in a handful of minutes.

Meal-prep thoughts: I wouldn't make the pizza ahead of time, but you can chop your chicken and all of your veggies and keep them in small Ziplocks to assemble your pizza for lunch all week.

grilled chicken and veggie rainbow bowl

WITH BLUE CHEESE, AVOCADO, AND WALNUTS

PREP: 10 MINUTES   TOTAL: 15 MINUTES   SERVES: 1

2 cups cauliflower rice (200 g)
2 green onions, chopped
Large pinch of cilantro
1 clove garlic (frozen cube)
1/4 cup brown rice (50 g)
3.5 oz grilled chicken (100 g)
About 1/4 cup grilled zucchini (45 g)
About 1/4 cup grilled onions (30 g)
Handful of cherry tomatoes (50 g)
1/4 of an avocado (30 g)
Sprinkle of reduced-fat blue cheese (10 g)
Pinch of toasted walnuts (5 g)
Fresh lime wedges

NOTES:

Rice: Trader Joe's frozen rice is a staple over here. If you've got plenty of carbs, skip the cauliflower rice and pile this in, of course!

Cauliflower: I suggest buying frozen just so you don't keep buying it and letting it rot and stink up your fridge! You can just cook as directed or jazz it up a little, like I do in the directions. Fresh cauliflower works, too--and you can even make your own by pulsing a fresh head of cauliflower in your food processor until rice-sized pieces form. But who's got time for that.

Other good additions: Grilled yellow squash and bell peppers are also good additions. And if you love dressing on everything, a drizzle of the Skinny Cilantro-Lime Ranch is great.

NUTRITION

Serving size: This bowl as described
384 Cal/11.8F/38C/36.5P

Search MFP for:
"Lillie Eats and Tells Grilled Chicken and Veggie Rainbow Bowl"

1. Make Cauliflower Rice: Sauté cauliflower rice with some green onions, cilantro, a frozen cube of garlic, and some S/P. You could just steam it--that works too.

2. Grill Veggies: Slice zucchini long ways into thick ribbons or spears for easy grilling. Slice onions in big rings, trying to keep together. Spray both with cooking spray, sprinkle with kosher salt/pepper, and grill for a couple of minutes per side (or until they've got good grill marks and have softened.) The onions might need to grill a bit longer. You can also use a grill pan inside. Chop veggies after grilled.

3. Assemble Bowl: Mix cauliflower and brown rice in bowl (I did 200g and 50g, but if I had plenty of carbs, I'd do all brown! Obviously if you'd like to decrease the carbs, you can use onlyl cauliflower rice (but a little chewy rice goes a long way for my carb-loving moral.)

4. Finish: Top with chopped grilled chicken, veggies, tomatoes, avocado, blue cheese, and toasted walnuts. Squeeze with lime (or feel free to add a drizzle of your favorite dressing!)

P.S. The blue cheese sounds so out of place, but I'm telling you, if you EVER like blue cheese, this is what MAKES THIS DISH! Such a weird, amazing combo. Especially with the real rice.

Walnuts: 5 grams is a TINY amount, but sometimes that's all the room I have, and it's still worth it! But by all means add more if you want! There is something about the rice, blue cheese, and walnut combo-- with the grilled flavor... I'm obsessed.

If you want to bulk it up even more, mix in your favorite salad greens.

Feeding the family: We like to lay out a spread of grilled meat and veggies, and everyone builds their own bowls. The little boys' might be very simple, but that leaves more for the rest of us!

Meal Prep: This is a great meal to pack ahead. Just becomes more of a grain salad.

peach and bacon flatbread

PREP: 10 MINUTES   TOTAL: 20 MINUTES   SERVES: 1

1 Greek Papa Pita
1 oz fresh mozzarella, grated or thinly sliced (28 g)
0.25 oz reduced fat blue cheese (7 g)
About 2 oz leftover grilled chicken (50 g)
1/3 of a peach, sliced thin (50 g)
1 piece of bacon
Red onion, sliced (20 g)
Arugula
Fresh basil
Balsamic drizzle (not included in macros)

NOTES:

Pitas: You can use Joseph's pitas from Walmart or Amazon for MUCH lower carbs--but occasionally I want to enjoy these big, fat, soft ones for a more substantial flatbread with my family.

Mozzarella: The fresh mozzarella packed in water is naturally a tiny bit lower in fat, probably because there's more moisture in it. But feel free to use grated.

Blue Cheese: I find the low-fat blue cheese in the Treasure Cave brand at Stater Brothers. Full-fat will add less than 1g fat per flatbread! No biggie.

Peaches: Apples or pears are great too when peaches aren't in season.

Bacon: I love Costco pre-cooked for ease! Still so good. Other pre-cooked options I've found never get crispy enough. Cooking raw bacon would be amazing, of course. But, don't you dare sub turkey bacon. Just kidding it's your flatbread--fine.

1. Preheat oven to 400 degrees.

2. Spray pita with a mist of olive oil spray and sprinkle with kosher salt.

3. Top with cheese, chicken, bacon, and onion.

4. Bake on a parchment-lined backing sheet for 5-8 minutes, until everything is melty and edges are browned. You want some crispiness!

5. Pull out and top with arugula, fresh basil, and a drizzle of balsamic glaze (I get mine at Trader Joe's.)

Feeding the Family: This is a favorite in our home because everyone can customize their own flatbread. I keep a basket in my freezer of shredded mozzarella and pepperoni so it doesn't go bad between "pizza nights." I whip that up with our favorite (and always on hand) marinara for the boys. My girls love Costco's jarred pesto with chicken and arugula. I can easily build mine on a large Joseph's lavash if I want to save more carbs. And, if I'm low on fats, I'll use low-fat mozzarella, or JUST the blue cheese.

Meal-prep thoughts: The flatbreads are so easy to assemble ahead and throw in the oven when everyone's ready.

Serve with a bowl of arugula for topping and some fruit for the kids!

NUTRITION

Serving size: 1 flatbread
437 Cal/13F/48C/31.7P/5.4 Fiber

Search MFP for:
"Lillie Eats and Tells Chicken, Bacon, Peach, and Blue Cheese Flatbread"

roasted tomato-basil chicken sandwich

WITH CARAMELIZED ONION, BACON, AND ARUGULA

• •

PREP: 20 MINUTES   TOTAL: 25 MINUTES

For the Sandwich (serves 1)
1 hollowed out Kaiser bun or "hard roll" (50 g)
4 oz pre-grilled chicken (113 g)
2 Tbs light basil garlic aioli
Roasted tomatoes (see below) (30 g)
1 slice of bacon
Arugula
Fresh basil
2 Tbs caramelized onion (see step 2)
1 slice extra-thinly sliced provolone or light provolone

For the Roasted Tomatoes (serves 6)
2 minced garlic cloves (or frozen cubes)
2 Tbs dried basil
1 tsp kosher salt
1 tsp fresh ground pepper
2 Tbs olive oil
6 roma tomatoes

NOTES:

Bread-logging tip: After the top is hollowed out, shoot for your kaiser roll to weight about 50 g. Search in MFP for "kaiser roll g" and compare a few until you've found one offered in grams that seems accurate, so that you can log 50.

Logging tomatoes and onions: They both shrink by about half when cooked, so as a general rule, if you use 30 g of cooked onions or tomatoes, you can log 60 g raw.

Save your leftover caramelized onions! I use them for pizzas, my favorite turkey burger, or any other flatbread, sandwich, wrap or pretty much anything. Such a flavor-maker.

1. **Roast tomatoes:** preheat oven to 425. Mix together everything but tomatoes. Quarter the tomatoes lengthwise and put in a big Ziplock with the marinade for five minutes. Line a baking sheet with foil and spray with cooking spray. Arrange tomatoes on the pan and roast for about 35 minutes (until they're blistered and super tender.) These are now ready to make EVERYTHING better.

2. **Caramelize onions** by sautéing thinly sliced onion (do 1/2-1 whole onion and use the leftovers!) over medium-low heat with a pinch of kosher salt and cooking spray for 20-30 minutes (until very tender). Stir occasionally.

3. If chicken is fresh off grill, quickly top two tenderloins with one slice of cheese and cover to melt. If using leftover chicken, place in warm oven OR broil just long enough for cheese to melt. The chicken doesn't need to be hot--that will make it taste reheated. **Just barely warmed** is great. Once it joins the fresh toasty bun and all of the other components, you'll never know it's leftover! As long as you don't OVER -heat.

4. Slice the bottom of your roll as thin as possible and hollow out the top. It will look uglier but save you carbs. AND, it will even make the sandwich BETTER because it leaves a nice, cozy spot for all of the toppings.

5. Spray the inside of the bun with olive oil spray and place face-down in a hot pan until golden brown. It's ok that the hollow part doesn't touch the pan.

6. Spread bun with basil garlic aioli. Top with cheesy chicken, roasted tomatoes, fresh basil, one slice of bacon, caramelized onion, arugula, and the top bun. ENJOY!

• •

P.S. Feeding the family: Lay your leftover chicken tenderloins on a sheet pan, drape with cheese and place it in the warm oven (after your tomatoes are done and while you prep everything else.) Toast buns on a pancake griddle to do lots at once. Let them customize their own sandwich! Mine love these.

Meal prep thoughts: You can make chicken, roasted tomatoes, caramelized onion, and basil garlic aioli ahead of time reheat on the same sheet pan then throw on toasted buns!

• •

mediterranean chicken flatbreads

PREP: 10 MINUTES   TOTAL: 15 MINUTES   SERVES: 1

2 Joseph's pitas
2.5 Tbs Trader Joe's Avocado Tzatziki (42 g)
3.5 oz leftover grilled chicken (100 g)
1 oz jarred roasted red peppers (28 g)
1/4 cup pickled onion* (30 g)
.5 oz fat-free feta (14 g) -I get mine at Trader Joe's
Hanfdul of cherry tomatoes halved (50 g)
Mixed greens
Fresh Lemon
Mint

NOTES:

Pitas: Sold at many Walmart or on Amazon. WORTH IT.

Feta: I find the fat-free feta at Trader Joe's

Tzatziki: This new version from Trader Joe's is delicious! But, their original is great, too! Or see the Greek pita recipe (on pg 29) for a homemade version.

NUTRITION

Serving size: 2 flatbreads
344 Cal/7.7F/30.2C/48.4P

To log, search MFP for:
"Lillie Eats and Tells Mediterranean Chicken Flatbreads"

1. Heat a non-stick pan to med-high, spray with cooking spray, and throw in some finely chopped or shredded chicken. Sprinkle with a little salt or garlic, if needed. Toss, after 30 seconds, and let it heat for just a minute or two total. JUST enough. Remove from pan and set aside.

2. Heat pita in same pan, spraying both sides with cooking spray and sprinkling with salt. Remove when hot and flexible. Try not to let it get too crispy and dry out.

3. Spread with avocado tzatziki. Top with chicken, roasted red peppers, pickled onion, feta, cherry tomatoes, greens, a pinch of fresh mint and a squeeze of fresh lemon. Enjoy!

P.S. I know this meal is very similar to the Greek pork pitas but I made them when I was in a time-pinch and wanted something similar, and was thrilled with how delicious and easy it was for a quick meal.

These pitas are boring and dry and cold, but really come alive if cooked right. Don't try and cook ahead of time. They're so much better fresh off the pan!

OR- you can bake in oven until crispy, and THEN top for a fresh Mediterranean pizza.

Feeding the family: Use the big soft Papa Pitas for your family. Everyone can top as they like!

Meal-prep thoughts: As long as your onions are pickled, everything else takes five minutes to throw together. You could pack it all in a bowl and keep the pitas separate to heat at work.

thai cauliflower fried rice

WITH CHICKEN AND FRESH HERBS

PREP: 20 MINUTES   TOTAL: 30 MINUTES   SERVES: 4-5

1/2 a medium onion, diced (100 g))
1 bell pepper, diced (145 g)
1 cup of frozen pea/carrot mixture (120 g)
12 oz cauliflower rice, fresh or frozen
1/2 tsp salt
2 cloves of garlic, minced (or frozen cubes)
2 Tbs ginger paste, or minced fresh ginger (30 g)
3 Tbs soy sauce
1 tsp honey (4 g)
1.5 Tbs sriracha hot sauce (22 g)
1 egg plus 1 egg white
1/2 cup shelled and cooked edamame (85 g)
10 oz grilled chicken, chopped (280 g)
2-3 green onions, chopped
Handful of cilantro, chopped (15 g)
Handful of fresh mint, chopped (10 g)
Extra sriracha and fresh lime for finishing

1. Heat a pan over medium-high heat. Spray with cooking spray (coconut oil spray if you have it.) Add onions, bell pepper, peas/carrots, riced cauliflower, and salt. Sauté for 5-6 minutes until veggies are aromatic and tender. If your cauliflower was frozen, you may need to cook longer to let the liquid cook off.

2. Add garlic, ginger paste, soy sauce, honey, and sriracha. Sauté for another 2 minutes. Push rice mixture to one side of the pan to make room for eggs.

3. Beat together your egg and egg white. Add them to the open spot on the pan to quickly scramble. Let eggs set a bit, but not dry out, then stir them well into the "rice" mixture so you'll have little bits of eggs througout.

4. Add edamame, grilled chicken, green onions, cilantro, and mint. Combine well and serve with a drizzle of sriracha and a squeeze of lime!

P.S. Additional yummy toppings: Avocado, mango, toasted peanuts or almonds, added fresh herbs, sriracha mayo (simply combine sriracha and lite mayo.) I even like it thrown on an Asian salad later! It's always nice to have something in the fridge that's just ready to go, already full of everything you need.

Feeding the family: You could combine theirs with a little added white rice and top with an extra fried egg!

Meal-prep thoughts: Great to make ahead and pack for lunch. Pair with lots of chopped butter lettuce and some Spicy Peanut Vinaigrette from Trader Joe's.

NUTRITION

Serving size: 225 g (about 2 cups)
240 Cal/5F/19C/29P

Search MFP for:
"Lillie Eats and Tells Thai Cauliflower Fried Rice with Chicken"

TURKEY-MUSHROOM MEATBALLS

THE PROTEIN

THE MEALS

turkey-mushroom meatballs

PREP: 20 MINUTES   TOTAL: 40 MINUTES   SERVES: 10-12

1 medium red bell pepper, roughly chopped (230 g)
1 small onion, roughly chopped (230 g)
10 cloves of garlic, minced (frozen Dorot cubes)
18 oz white mushrooms+salt and pepper
1/4-1/2 cup fresh parsley (optional)
1 Tbs kosher salt
2 tsp pepper
1 Tbs cumin
1.5 tsp crushed fennel (optional)
1.5 tsp dried oregano
About 2 slices of white bread (100 g)
1 egg, lightly beaten
4 lbs extra-lean 99/1 ground turkey
Red pepper flakes (optional)

NOTES:

These meatballs can be tossed in marinara, buffalo, hoisin, peanut, or teriyaki sauce. We like to keep the base mild enough and treat it as a meal-prep protein that can be used in a variety of ways.

Fennel: I used to think I hated fennel. It has that black licorice thing happening. But, it makes these meatballs taste more like italian sausage, and is a game-changer for me! If you're unsure you can sprinkle a few tops to try it out. Or, choose to only add it later when using the meatballs in an Italian dish.

NUTRITION

Serving size: 150 g baked meatballs (8-9 small meatballs)
157 Cal/2F/8C/26.5P

Search MFP for:
"Lillie Eats and Tells Turkey Mushroom Meatballs"

1. **Cook the mushrooms:** Wipe mushrooms clean, trim any gross ends, quarter, and sauté in a pan with cooking spray, a big pinch of kosher salt and pepper over medium-high heat, until soft.

2. **Make breadcrumbs:** Put two slices of white bread (or 100 g) into a food processor or blender. Pulse until rough crumbs are formed. Remove and set aside.

3. **Blend or process the ugly but delicious mixture**: Add (to that same food processor or blender) the chopped bell pepper, onion, garlic, sautéed mushrooms, parsley, and spices. Process until smooth. Throw in the bread crumbs and pulse a few more times. Add egg (making sure the mixture is not too warm at this point) and process one last time.

4. **Combine mushroom mixture and raw ground turkey** in a large bowl. Use your hands, if it doesn't scare you, to combine everything thoroughly.

5. **Make the meatballs:** Pre-heat oven to 425. Using a 1 Tbs cookie scoop, form balls and line them up on the pan. They can be pretty close but not touching. Sprinkle the tops with another layer of kosher salt. If you like heat, add some red pepper flakes. I never mix them in because of my kids. Bake for 18-20 minutes until cooked through. You can refigerate or freeze for later, or continue with step 6.

6. **Pan-fry:** Whether they're fresh from the oven or cold from the fridge, heat a skillet to medium-high heat, spray with cooking spray, and sear meatballs quickly on all sides, adding any additional sauces or seasonings depending on your meal. This gives them better texture, color, and flavor!

P.S. I love to use a cookie scoop for my meatballs. It makes my job easier AND I actually prefer the flat bottoms for sandwich building. Of course if you don't have a cookie scoop, you can use a spoon and roll into balls, but the mixture will be very soft and sticky. Wet hands will help with that, but a few dollars on a cookie scoop will change your meatball-making life!

For logging purposes it doesn't matter how big you make your meatballs since you'll just weigh your final baked meatball portion and log in grams. You may just need to bake longer if you do larger meatballs. Mine were done with my 1-Tbs cookie scoop and were just about 17 g a piece.

classic meatball subs

PREP: 10 MINUTES   TOTAL: 15 MINUTES   SERVES: 1

3.5 oz cooked turkey mushroom meatballs (100 g or
   about 6 small meatballs)

1 hollowed out baguette or other roll (60 g)

1/4 cup marinara

1 oz lite provolone cheese (28g)

1 Tbs light basil garlic aioli (15 g)- pg 12

NOTES:

Bread: The macros on bread are all SO close when
you're dealing with the same weigh. If you use 60 g of
bread you'll be close enough, even if it's a different
bread.

Marinara: Our favorite marinara is the Victoria's Organic Marinara from Costco. 6 carbs per serving and it's
delicious. Feel free to use your favorite.

NUTRITION

Serving size: 1 sandwich with 100g meatballs
388 Cal/6.5F/45.6C/34.7P

Search MFP for:
"Lillie Eats and Tells Classic Turkey Mushroom
Meatball Subs"

1. Pre-heat broiler. Slice baguette and hollow out as much as
you can. Lay just the tops (or whichever half has a better
divet for your meatballs) face up on a baking sheet, spray
with olive oil spray, sprinkle with garlic salt, and broil for a
minute or two until slightly golden.

2. Fill the toasted hollowed-out half with meatballs, top with
sauce, then cheese. Add the bottom buns to the cookie
sheet, mist with olive oil spray, and sprinkle with garlic salt.
Broil the sheet pan again for a couple of minutes until the
bottom buns are golden and the cheese on the meatballs is
melted.

3. Pull out your pan, spread the bottom bun with basil garlic
aioli, and put your sandwich together! Sometimes I add arugula for crunch and volume! Enjoyyyyy.

P.S. I like to cut the bottom as thin as I can and then pull out
as much of the inside as possible. This gets the weight down
and reduces the carbs without losing any flavor. This crusty
baguette really compliments a soft meatball well, but we
love these on just about anything. The hollow works better
on slightly airier sandwich rolls like the bolillos we typically
use for sandwiches. A kaiser bun works great too. It's light
and airy and easy to hollow out the top and get it pretty light
while still having a good surface area to work with for a good
sized sandwich. You just build your sandwich in the shape of
a hamburger instead of a sub.

If you can find a brioche hot dog bun (Aldi sells some) or Hawaiian sweet roll hot dog buns; they're not good to hollow
out (that would destroy them) but they're really yummy and
can make perfect smaller sandwiches. They're also easy to
build with the split top. (See Buffalo meatball sub recipe.)

Feeding the family: This one is a favorite with my family.

Meal-prep thoughts: Have meatballs and aioli made in advance and throwing the sandwich together is a breeze!
Meatballs are great, thawed out of the freezer.

coconut-curried turkey meatballs

OVER ZOODLES

PREP: 20 MINUTES   TOTAL: 30 MINUTES   SAUCE SERVES: 6-8

For the Coconut-Curry Sauce: (serves 6-8)
1/2 medium onion, diced (100 g)
3 cloves of garlic, minced (or frozen cubes)
1.5 Tbs ginger paste (or grated fresh)
1 Tbs garam masala
2 tsp mild curry powder
1/2 tsp turmeric
1/2 tsp cayenne pepper (optional)
2 Tbs tomato paste (30 g)
5 oz jarred marinara
12 oz Califia Farms Toasted Coconut Almond
  Milk (or sub regular almond milk)
1 small container Dannon Light and Fit Toasted
  Coconut Vanilla Greek yogurt (150g)

For the Bowl: (serves 1)
2 medium zucchini, spiralized (250 g)
9 small turkey-mushroom meatballs (150 g)
1/2 cup coconut curry (recipe above) (75 g)
Cilantro
Lime
Sliced sweet mini bell peppers

NOTES:

Favorite jarred marinara: Ours is Victoria's Organic from Costco. Trader Joe's Rustico is a good second with almost identical macros.

Zucchini: Weigh and log before you salt or cook it. It will shrink, but you'll still be eating the full 250 grams of raw zucchini.

NUTRITION

Serving size: This bowl as described
250 Cal/4.3F/22.3C/32.3P

Search MFP for:
"Lillie Eats and Tells Coconut Curried Turkey Meatballs over Zoodles" OR "coconut curry" to log curry on it's own.

1. Make the sauce: Cook your onion over medium heat with cooking spray for about five minutes, until fragrant.

Add garlic and ginger and cook another 3 minutes. Add spices and tomato paste and stir around to wake it all up before adding liquid. It'll be wierd and thick--that's okay.

Stir in marinara and almond milk and let it come to a LOW boil for about 2 to 3 minutes to thicken a bit. Whisk in coconut yogurt and turn off heat. Keep covered until ready to serve.

2. Make your zoodles: Sprinkle zoodles with kosher salt and let sit in a colander in your sink for about 5 minutes to get rid of some of the water. Rinse, pat and gently squeeze with paper towels to dry.

Over medium-high heat, sauté your spiralized zucchini in cooking spray (coconut oil spray ideally) for about 3 minutes.

3. Assemble your bowl: Pile zoodles in your bowl. Top with 150 g meatballs (9 meatballs, in my case!) and 75 g of the sauce. Garnish with cilantro and sliced sweet peppers, jalapenos, or serrano chilis. Green onions would be great too. Squeeze with fresh lime.

P.S. These would be great served over cauliflower rice, spaghetti squash, or steamed rice.

This meal is so light! There's plenty of room for a Joseph's pita on the side to act like naan. For tracking purposes you can search this bowl as described or you can search the "Lillie Eats and Tells Coconut Curry" and the "Turkey Mushroom Meatballs" separately.

Feeding the family: Hopefully they like curry. My kids will have rice! If you're unsure about the strong flavors, start lighter on the spices and taste as you go. The sauce seems to mellow out in the fridge for later.

Meal-prep thoughts: The curry can be frozen alone or with meatballs for later use! Just thaw and heat in pan.

buffalo meatball subs

WITH CRISP CABBAGE AND TANGY BLUE CHEESE

PREP: 10 MINUTES   TOTAL: 15 MINUTES   SERVES: 1

9 small turkey-mushroom meatballs (150 g)
Frank's RedHot® Sauce
1 tsp reduced-fat blue cheese
2 Hawaiian hot dog buns
Bagged coleslaw or shredded cabbage
1/2 Tbs Bolthouse Ranch or Blue Cheese dressing (7g)
Green onions, chopped

NOTES:

Buns: Obviously any bun will work, but I loved how the sweet bun compliments the spicy hot sauce--and I love how they're split on top.

Blue cheese: If you can't find reduced-fat blue cheese, just use the real stuff. It's such a tiny portion, it will hardly make a difference, but adds so much flavor!

Can't fit the carbs? Just have just one flatbread and pile the rest of the meatballs on a salad. You could also swap the buns for some Joseph's pitas.

NUTRITION

Serving size: 2 subs with 150 g meatballs total
442 Cal/9.5F/54.4C/35.6P

Search MFP for:
"Lillie Eats and Tells Buffalo Turkey Mushroom Meatball Subs"

1. Pre-heat broiler for step 5.

2. Heat a pan over medium-high heat on your stovetop with some cooking spray. Add meatballs and let sit 30-60 seconds on each side to get some color.

3. Pour about 1/4 cup Frank's RedHot Sauce in a bowl (however much you need.) Remove meatballs from pan once they've browned and toss them in the sauce so they're covered.

4. Put meatballs back in the pan, sprinkle with blue cheese, and cover for a minute to melt a bit.

5. Place your buns on a baking sheet (trying to open them up) with a fine mist of olive oil or other cooking spray. Sprinkle lightly with garlic salt. Broil for a few minutes until golden brown.

6. Line up three meatballs per bun, add some cabbage, a pinch of green onions, and a drizzle of ranch or blue cheese dressing. Enjoy!

P.S. Macro pro-tip: If you need to scrape off a few carbs but want two sandwiches like I always do, you can carefully shave off a thin layer of bread on both sides leaving a smaller, lighter bun. Weigh your final product and compare to what the label says it should be. For instance, if it's supposed to be a 37 g bun and yours is now 26, you can divide 26 by 37 to find that you have 0.7 of a bun. Maybe now you can fit two!

Feeding the family: For our younger two, we skip the hot sauce combo and just do some jarred marinara.

Meal-prep thoughts: The meatballs are a great pack-and-go option for lunch. Maybe just add some rice or cauliflower rice in place of a bun to make it a buffalo meatball bowl.

meatball flatbreads

PREP: 10 MINUTES   TOTAL: 15 MINUTES   SERVES: 1

2 Joseph's pitas

1/4 cup marinara

1 oz fresh mozzarella cheese (28 g)

9 small turkey-mushroom meatballs (150 g)

Pinch of red pepper flakes

Handful of arugula

Fresh lemon

NOTES:

The pitas: Sometimes they can be quite a bit off in weight, which means the macros would be higher than listed. If you want to be very accurate, weigh yours and log the extra. Or, carefully peel away part of the second layer to get it close to the 37 g.

Marinara: Our favorite is the Victoria's Organic Marinara from Costco. 6 carbs per serving, and it's delicious. The Trader Joe's Rustico is good too, with similar macros.

Mozzarella: I use full-fat packed in water if I can afford the macros. It's slightly lower in fat than a full-fat grated, because it has more water in it. I love the flavor and how it melts but feel free to use low-fat and log your flatbread by component.

NUTRITION

Serving size: Two flatbreads
381 Cal/12F/31.7C/45.4P

Search MFP for:
"Lillie Eats and Tells Meatball Flatbreads with Arugula"

1. Heat oven to 475' and line a baking sheet with parchment paper. (Or you can spray your pan with non-stick spray.)

2. Lay your pitas on the lined pan, top each with marinara, thinly sliced fresh mozzarella, and 75 g of meatballs crumbled or cut into halves. Sprinkle with a pinch of red pepper flakes and kosher salt and spray with a mist of olive oil spray.

3. Bake for 6-8 minutes (or until the edges of the pita are brown and crispy.) Remove from oven. Toss arugula in lemon juice and top pizza. The lemon is key!

P.S. Of course you can watch your flatbread and take it out whenever you prefer, but for pizzas I really feel like these pitas pick up a much better flavor when they're nice and crispy.

Feeding the family: We always keep the big Papa Pitas on hand too, and I build everyone else's flatbreads on those. They're delicious, and it's easy to pull out some pepperoni for the boys.

Meal-prep thoughts: You can assemble these ahead of time and then throw on the pan to cook. Or even save leftovers to cook again. Leave off arugula, of course. You can also reheat your flatbread in a pan over medium-high heat until it's warm and crispy.

thai sweet chili meatball bowl

PREP: 15 MINUTES   TOTAL: 25 MINUTES   SERVES: 1

For the Spaghetti Squash:
2 cups spaghetti squash, cooked (300 g)
2 Tbs soy sauce
1/2- 1 whole fresh lime, juiced
Handful of cilantro, chopped

For the Meatballs:
6 small turkey-mushroom meatballs (100 g)
Sprinkle of garlic powder
1 Tbs sweet chili sauce

Additional items for the Bowl:
1/4 cup carrots, thinly sliced (30 g)
1/4 cup bell pepper, cut into matchsticks (30 g)
1/4 cup cucumber, sliced thin (30 g)
2 Tbs radishes, cut into little matchsticks
2 Tbs green onions, chopped
Big pinch of chopped mint leaves
Jalapeño, chopped
Salt and pepper
Top with your favorite Asian dressing (not included in macros. Use what you want!)

NOTES:

I love a vegetable peeler to ribbon cucumbers and carrots. You can also spiralize them or just cut in matchsticks. I prefer a noodley shape for this.

Dressing: My favorite is the Spicy Peanut Vinaigrette from Trader Joe's. I love the Newman's Own Sesame Ginger too. Stir in a little powdered peanut butter if you'd like a peanut dressing.

NUTRITION

Serving size: This bowl as described
307 Cal/5.4F/44.2C/22.4P

Search MFP for:
"Lillie Eats and Tells Thai Sweet Chili Meatball Bowl"

1. **Cook spaghetti squash:** You can use your favorite method, but I just poke mine 5 times and microwave for 6-8 minutes, turning halfway through. When the skin is tender, pull it out and carefully cut off stemmed end. Stand it up to cut in half lengthwise. Scoop out the seedy/mushy middle, and using a fork, pull the rest of the squash out in strings. Set aside.

2. **Sauté squash with cilantro:** Heat a pan over medium-high heat. Spray with coconut oil spray (ideal for the flavor addition.) Add spaghetti squash, a pinch of salt and pepper, soy sauce and juice from a lime. Sauté for 2-3 minutes. Stir in a big handful of fresh chopped cilantro.

3. **Coat and cook the meatballs:** Sprinkle meatballs with a little garlic powder and kosher salt. Cook in a pre-heated and sprayed skillet over medium-high heat for a couple of minutes to brown. Remove from pan and toss around in a bowl with 1 Tbs sweet chili sauce. Return meatballs to the pan and cook for another minute to caramelize. Make sure to drag the meatballs through any gooey, sugary bits in the pan to get all the good stuff stuck to the meatballs.

4. **Build Bowl:** Add spaghetti squash to a bowl, top with meatballs, carrots, bell pepper, cucumber, green onions, radishes, fresh mint, jalapeno, a couple of tablespoons of your dressing, and a big squeeze of fresh lime. Enjoy!

P.S. Sweet chili sauce: I buy mine at Trader Joe's because it's the lowest in carbs I've found (6 instead of 10 per Tbs.) You can find it at any grocery store near the bbq sauces and usually in any Asian food section. One tablespoon is not much because I didn't want to let the carbs climb; it's just enough to give it the delicious sweet caramelized exterior! But if you've got carbs to spare, double up. If you decide to dip each meatball in a bowl of the sweet chili sauce, they'll pick up about 5 grams each, bringing this to 2 Tbs total.

Meal-prep thoughts: Chop the veggies and cook the squash ahead of time. Heat the squash and meatballs and top with fresh veggies, etc. You could even add greens and eat it totally cold as a salad.

Feeding the family: My girls love it with linguini or rice noodles, so it's more like a Thai noodle salad.

INSTANT POT (OR SLOW COOKER) SHREDDED CHICKEN

smoky honey-cilantro chicken

12 MINUTES IN THE INSTANT POT

PREP: 15 MINUTES   TOTAL: 30 MINUTES   SERVES: 8–10

1 cup salsa verde

1 small white onion, chopped (200 g)

2 Tbs honey

1 Tbs liquid smoke

5 cloves of garlic (frozen cubes)

2 tsp chili powder

1.5 tsp kosher salt

1 tsp dried oregano

1 tsp cumin

½ tsp paprika

2-3 lbs chicken tenderloins

NUTRITION

Serving size: 113 g shredded chicken
115 Cal/1.5F/6C/21P

Search MFP for:
"Lillie Eats and Tells Instant Pot Smokey Honey Cilantro Chicken"

1. Mix together everything but the chicken.

2. Combine sauce and chicken in instant pot. Close and set to manual for 12 minutes. Seal valve. It will take a while to reach the pressure and start the timer, so it will actually take closer to 30 minutes. When done, let the steam release naturally for ten minutes (or so) and then open the vent and lid. (If it's hard to open, wait a few more minutes. No biggie here.)

3. Shred, toss it around in the juices, and stir in ½ cup chopped fresh cilantro.

P.S. You can use fresh or frozen tenderloins! 12 minutes is stil fine. If you double it, cook for 15 minutes.

This is one of my favorite instant pot recipe. Adapted from Mels Kitchen Cafe. So easy and delicious, it's ready to build a number of meals!

Slow Cooker Instructions: Put everything in slow cooker on low until tender (about 6-7 hours). Shred, stir in fresh cilantro.

Meal-prep thoughts: This is a great bulk protein, like all of the others! Keep some in fridge to use all week, and some in the freezer for a busy week! Let thaw and reheat as needed in a slow cooker, a hot pan, broiler, or even just for a short time in the microwave. This shredded, flavorful meat is so forgiving.

chipotle-lime shredded chicken

PREP: 10 MINUTES   TOTAL: 30 MINUTES   SERVES: 8–10

2 lbs chicken tenderloins (breasts work too)

1/2 cup jarred red salsa

5 cloves of garlic, minced (or frozen cubes)

1 Tbs liquid smoke

1-2 Tbs chipotle peppers in adobo sauce, minced

2 Tbs lime juice (1 lime juiced)

2 tsp garlic powder

2 tsp onion powder

1 tsp cumin

1 tsp chili powder

1.5 tsp kosher salt

1/4 tsp pepper

NOTES:

Salsa: Try and choose a basic 2 carbs/2 Tbs salsa option--any will work! We love the double roasted from Trader Joe's.

Chipotle Peppers in Adobo Sauce: You can also throw the whole can in the food processor and measure from that. Store the remaining in the fridge to make frequent batches of chipotle cream!

1. Place thawed chicken in the bottom of instant pot.

2. Add everything else on top! Don't even bother dirtying another dish--just get it all in there.

3. Toss it around a bit. Hit manual and set your timer for 12 minutes at high pressure. (When I'm using breasts I like to do 30. They'll cook in 15 minutes, but there's nothing worse than tough breasts for me.) Close, seal, and walk away.

4. Let it naturally release for 10 minutes, or so. Then open and shred. Use two forks and your muscles to shred. Once shredded, give it good toss in its juices. You shouldn't really have any liquid to discard after you get it all shredded and moved around to soak back up the flavor.

P.S. I find chicken tenderloins to shred much easier than breasts. You can even put them in completely frozen. Don't even change the time! If you double the recipe, cook for 15 minutes. For breasts (fresh or frozen), I prefer to cook for 30 minutes.

For Slow Cooker: Place all ingredients in a slow cooker and add 1/2 cup chicken stock or water since the liquid can dry up in the slow cooker. Cook on low for 4- 5 hours.

Meal-prep thoughts: make a bunch of chicken--use some all week and freeze some for later!

NUTRITION

Serving size: 100 g shredded chicken
108 Cal/1F/3C/21P

Search MFP for:
"Lillie Eats and Tells Chipotle Lime Instant Pot Taco Chicken"

creamy buffalo chicken

PREP: 10 MINUTES   **TOTAL:** 45 MINUTES   **SERVES:** 10

2 lbs chicken breast (about 3 fresh breasts)

1 small onion, diced (200 g)

6 cloves of garlic, minced (or frozen cubes)

1 cup Frank's RedHot sauce

1/4 cup chicken stock (or water)

1 Tbs ranch seasoning

1/2 Tbs Italian seasoning

3 oz Greek cream cheese (or reduced-fat cream cheese)

Fresh parsley

I usually prefer tenderloins, but breasts have turned out great in this recipe, and sometimes feel so easy! If you use tenderloins, you only need to cook for 12 minutes.

NUTRITION

Serving size: 100 g chicken
114 Cal/2.8F/3.5C/18.6P

Search MFP for:
"Lillie Eats and Tells Creamy Buffalo Chicken"

1. Spray bottom of instant pot with cooking spray, add breasts, onion, garlic, hot sauce, water, Italian and ranch seasonings. Close lid; close vent. Set on manual high pressure for 30 minutes.

2. Allow the steam to naturally release. Open and shred the chicken nice and fine, so it really asborbs the juices. You can use your stand or hand mixer to shred, but I've found this to be a breeze with two forks and no extra dishes. Turn the instant pot to "sauté" setting and let cook for 10 more minutes (or until liquid is reduced and absorbed, stirring often). Turn off heat. Add Greek cream cheese and fresh parsely, and stir until the cream cheese melts and it's all well-combined. There shouldn't be any liquid remaining. Use for taquitos, sandwiches, sweet potatoes, pizzas, etc!

For slow cooker: Place chicken in the slow cooker. Top with onions, garlic, Frank's hot sauce, 1/2 cup water or chicken stock (TWICE what the recipe calls for) and seasonings. Combine. Cook on low for 6-7 hours or on high for 4-6 hours until chicken is easy to shred. Shred chicken and toss around in the juices to soak up as much as you can. Discard excess liquid and stir in cream cheese and parsley.

buffalo chicken stuffed sweet potato

PREP: 10 MINUTES   TOTAL: 1 HOUR   SERVES: 1

1 small sweet potato (200 g)
4.5 oz shredded buffalo chicken (125 g)
1 tsp crumbled reduced-fat blue cheese (4 g)
Green onion, chopped
Frank's RedHot sauce, drizzled
Walden Farms Maple Walnut Syrup, drizzled
1.5 Tbs chipotle cream (20 g)---pg 12
Cilantro, chopped

NOTES:

Walden Farms Syrup: Seems strange, but I love the sweet drizzle with the spicy chicken! Feel free to use and track your favorite low sugar syrup. The Walden Farms is calorie-free. (Please don't mistake that for my saying it's "healthy!")

Extra toppings: I love to add avocado, chopped sweet bell peppers, pickled onions (because obviously I add them to everything,) and lots of greens. I highly recommend adding avocado! Your favorite ranch or blue cheese dressing would also be great.

1. Preheat oven to 425. Wash and dry potatoes. Spray with olive oil spray and rub it all over the potatoes with your hands. Sprinkle liberally with course salt and poke 5 or 6 times with a sharp knife to allow steam to escape. Place on cooling rack set on a cookie sheet. You might want to line your pan with foil for easy clean-up. Bake for 45-50 minutes until tender.

2. Cut a slit in the top of the hot potato and squeeze the ends toward each other to open it up. Drizzle chipotle cream inside sweet potato and stuff with warm buffalo chicken.

3. Top with crumbled blue cheese, (avocado if adding), green onions, cilantro, extra hot sauce, and Walden Farms Maple Walnut Syrup if you don't think I've gone crazy! I also love pickled onions on mine, but that's no suprise.

P.S. Feeding the family: Bake as many potatoes as you have eaters! I'm just listing ingredients and macros for one serving for tracking ease. Serve with a nice green salad.

Meal-prep thoughts: This is an easy meal to pack to go. Just reheat potato and chicken and add toppings.

NUTRITION

Serving size: 1 stuffed 200 g potato
344 Cal/4.6F/47.6C/28.6P

Search MFP for:
"Lillie Eats and Tells Buffalo Chicken Stuffed Sweet Potatoes"

baked buffalo chicken taquitos

WITH AVOCADO MASH AND BLUE CHEESE CRUMBLES

PREP: 10 MINUTES   TOTAL: 30 MINUTES   SERVES: 1

1 Cut Da Carb (or other low-carb wrap)
5.5 oz creamy buffalo chicken (160 g)
2 Tbs skinny chipotle cream (30 g)-- pg 12
Fresh herbs (cilantro, parsley, chives)
1/4 a small avocado (30 g)
1 Tbs Bolthouse Ranch or Blue Cheese dressing (15 g)
2 tsp reduced-fat blue cheese crumbles (8 g)
Shredded lettuce
Sweet mini bell peppers, diced
Franks RedHot Sauce

NOTES:

Wrap: So I LOVE the Cut Da Carb and use those most often. But, the Joseph's lavash works great too. They're just a little thicker and I feel like they require a little more dipping- but that's fine! I'll include an option to track with either.

Blue cheese: It can be hard to find the low-fat blue cheese by Treasure Cave. I find it at Stater Bros., but if you love blue cheese and can't find it, just use full-fat and it will only add about ONE gram of fat to your portion. No biggie!

I warned you that we eat the chipotle cream on everything!

NUTRITION

Serving size: 4 topped taquitos
383 Cal/13F/27C/40P OR:

4 taquitos with no toppings:
290 Cal/6F/23C/37P

Search MFP for:
"Lillie Eats and Tells Baked Buffalo Chicken Taquitos" OR to log them without toppings, search "Lillie Eats and Tells Naked Baked Buffalo Chicken Taquitos"

1. Preheat oven to 450.

2. Cut your Cut Da Carb or Joseph's lavash wrap into fourths. Add 40 g (about 1/4 cup) of creamy chicken mixture to each rectangle, about 8 g of skinny chipotle cream, and a pinch of fresh herbs if using. Roll up from the long side into a taquito.

3. Place on parchment-lined baking sheet (or spray pan because they'll stick,) seam down. Spray tops with cooking spray and sprinkle with kosher salt. Bake for 10 minutes, then flip and bake for another 10 or until browned and crisp on each side. They won't get totally crispy, but we still love them.

4. Plate four taquitos and top with 30 g mashed avocado, 8 g crumbled blue cheese, shredded lettuce, a pinch of diced sweet bell peppers, a tablespoon of your dressing, and a little extra drizzle of Frank's RedHot sauce. Enjoy!

P.S. You can also add the blue cheese inside the taquitos, but I wanted this to be super easy.

Feeding the family: Build the rest of the taquitos in flour tortillas. They're amazing like that. Corn tortillas are good too, but flour creates a really good texture.

Meal-prep thoughts: These taquitos can be frozen and baked later! Just wrap tightly in foil and store in a big Ziploc so they won't unravel.

chipotle-lime chicken tacos

PREP: 10 MINUTES   TOTAL: 15 MINUTES   SERVES: 1

3 Extra-Thin Mission corn tortillas

5.25 oz chipotle lime shredded chicken (150 g)

1.5 Tbs skinny chipotle cream (20 g)-- pg 12

1/4 of a small avocado (20 g)

2 Tbs mango, diced (20 g)

Pinch of quick pickled onion (15 g)-- pg 15

Large pinch of fresh cilantro

1 tsp cotija (5 g)

NOTES:

Tortillas: I find the extra-thin corn tortillas at Ralph's and Walmart. Don't stress if you can't find them. Just compare some labels to find the lowest in carbs that you can (if you want lower carbs.) I don't find the tiny street tacos to be better macros unless I only eat three, and they're so small. Consider size and macros and log the ones you find. Corn is generally going to be lighter in all areas than a similarly-sized flour tortilla.

NUTRITION

Serving size: 3 tacos
376Cal/8F/37C/38P

Search MFP for:
"Lillie Eats and Tells Chipotle Lime Chicken Tacos"

1. Heat tortillas in a pan over medium-high heat with a mist of cooking spray until hot.

2. Top with shredded chicken, chipotle cream, avocado, mango, pickled onions, a big pinch of fresh cilantro, and a sprinkle of cotija cheese. Enjoy!

P.S. If you like your tortillas charred like in this photo, just put them right on the burner and flip, after a minute, with tongs.

Feeding the family: My family loves tacos! These can be as simple as you want.

Meal-prep thoughts: I hope by now you've got chipotle cream, and pickled onions hanging out in your fridge. Ha. If so these are such a breeze at dinner time.

skinny creamy chicken enchiladas

PREP: 20 MINUTES   TOTAL: 40 MINUTES   SERVES: 4–6

2.5 oz fat-free cream cheese (70 g)

1/4 cup salsa verde (60 g)

1 Tbs lime juice

1/2 tsp cumin

1 tsp chili powder

1/2 tsp onion powder

1/4 tsp garlic powder

1/3 cup cilantro

3 Tbs green onions, chopped

2 cups of shredded smokey honey-cilantro chicken (500 g)

16 Extra-Thin Mission corn tortillas

1 cup Trader Joe's bottled red enchilada sauce

3 oz lite shredded Mexican cheese blend (84 g)

Additional recommended toppings (not included in macros):

Avocado, fat-free sour cream or Greek yogurt, pico , and cotija cheese should all find themselves on top!

NOTES:

Cream Cheese: I often prefer to use whipped Greek cream cheese, which would add 2 fat per serving.

Chicken: If you have enough chicken feel free to double filling recipe for later! It freezes great and is perfect for baked taquitos, like the recipe from Our Best Bites.

NUTRITION

Serving size: 4 enchiladas with sauce and cheese
417 Cal/8.5F/47.8C/37.7P

Search MFP for:
"Lillie Eats and Tells Skinny Creamy Chicken Enchiladas"

1. Weigh your bowl before you combine the chicken mixture and make a note of the weight.

2. Microwave your cream cheese for about 20-30 seconds, until soft. Mix in salsa, lime juice, and all the dry seasonings. Stir in cilantro, green onion, and chicken. (I do this in my Kitchenaid, so it tears my chicken apart for me.) Now weigh the final chicken mixture, subtracting the weight of the bowl. Divide that by your 16 tortillas.

3. Warm your corn tortillas in an open Ziploc for 20-30 seconds (until they're flexible). Put the 1/16th portion of chicken mixture in each tortilla and roll it up. (Mine was around 40 grams.) Line up, seam-side down, in a greased 9x13 pan.

4. Cover with sauce and shredded cheese. Bake at 425 until cheese is melty (about 10-15 minutes.)

The macros stop there, but I hope you top with lite sour cream, pico, avocado, and cotija.

P.S. I bought these darling mini dishes, so I could make mine and Ross's perfect for us but I've re-written this recipe to be made in a 9x13.

If you're not already buying cotija I swear it brings every mexican dish to life. A little goes a long way.

Tips: I always put my whole big dish on the scale and work on that. Put one tortilla in the dish, zero out the scale. Add chicken to 40 g, zero out the scale, and do it again and again. This way you're not measuring chicken in several bowls.

Feeding the family: Your family will love these! And if you make two pans, you can pile more cheese on theirs just to be sure.

Meal-prep thoughts: This is a delicious make-ahead meal to eat all week! You can also assemble enchiladas and freeze for baking later. Leave out to thaw and pop in the oven for the same time.

mexican spaghetti squash boats

PREP: 10 MINUTES   TOTAL: 15 MINUTES   SERVES: 1

1 small spaghetti squash (320 g)
3.5 oz cilantro or chipotle instant pot chicken (100 g)
1/4 cup pico de gallo (50 g)--pg13
1/4 of a small avocado (30 g)
1.5 Tbs creamy cilantro-lime ranch (20 g)--pg 14
2 Tbs skinny chipotle cream (30 g)--pg 12
2 tsp cotija cheese (8 g)

NOTES:

If you track macros: Steamed and raw spaghetti squash are not that different in macros because not too much moisture is lost. If you sauté your squash, to pull out the moisture, that's when it'll shrink and become more calorie-dense. Weigh your portion after roasting or steaming if you're ever going to sauté it after that. (Sautéeing is not necessary in this recipe.)

Cotija: Cotija cheese is such a game changer to me with Mexican food--a little goes so far and adds so much flavor. If you can't find it, feta is a good alternative.

Cilantro-Lime Ranch: Bolthouse Cilantro Avocado is a great store-bought option; or, just use some light sour cream if you like things more classic.

NUTRITION

Serving size: 320 g spaghetti squash plus toppings
349 Cal/9.2F/33.2C/38.4P

Search MFP for:
"Lillie Eats and Tells Mexican Spaghetti Squash Boats"

1. Cook spaghetti squash however you'd like. I love to roast it cut side down, like Martha, but, for this quick meal, I just microwave it. Poke it a few times and put the whole thing in for 5-8 minutes (or until it's tender and you can squeeze it.)

2. Cut in half and carefully spoon out the seedy center, trying not to waste a bunch of the squash.

3. Use a fork to pull the squash from the skin and form the strings. Put a bowl on your scale and throw the squash in to weigh your portion. Toss with a little salt and pepper and your chipotle cream. Put it back in the skin.

4. Top with chicken, avocado, and pico. Drizzle with dressing and a sprinkle of cotija. Finish with salt and pepper and some extra cilantro.

P.S. If you'd rather roast the squash, you can cut in half or microwave for two minutes to soften a little for cutting.; Spoon out the seeds, mist with olive oil spray and season with salt and pepper. Place both halves cut side down on a foil-lined baking sheet and roast at 425 for 45-60 minutes, depending on size. It's done when the skin is tender. This is definitely my favorite way to cook spaghetti squash when I've got the time.

Feeding the family: I like to microwave some quick Trader Joe's brown rice to serve as the base for any kids who don't love spaghetti squash, or throw the toppings in a quesadilla.

Meal-prep thoughts: This is an easy meal to pack. Just package the cold items separately to add on after you reheat the squash and chicken. My favorite way to reheat the chicken is in a hot pan for just a COUPLE of minutes--long enough to take the cold out, but not long enough to taste reheated!

shredded chicken lavash nachos

PREP: 10 MINUTES   TOTAL: 15 MINUTES   SERVES: 1

1.5 Joseph's lavash

1 oz lite three cheese Mexican blend (28 g)

2 Tbs Trader Joe's jarred queso (30 g)

2 tsp cotija cheese (10 g)

3.5 oz shredded instant pot chicken (100 g)

1/2-3/4 cup fresh quick homemade pico (100 g)--pg 13

1/2 a small avocado (40 g)

2 Tbs homemade cilantro-lime ranch (30 g) --pg 14

2 Tbs fresh mango, diced (30 g)

Plenty of extra cilantro

NOTES:

Cheese: Trader Joe's lite Mexican cheese blend is my favorite shredded low-fat cheese.

Queso: Feel free to use another jarred queso if you'd like. Trader Joe's queso just has no fat!

Dressing: Bolthouse Cilantro Avocado is a great store-bought option, or just use some light sour cream if you like things more classic.

NUTRITION

Serving size: 1 whole pan
575 Cal/20F/55C/56P

Search MFP for:
"Lillie Eats and Tells Personal Pan of Macro Friendly Nachos"

1. Chop your lavash into chip-sized triangles and lay out on a foil-lined baking sheet, or pizza pan. Spray with cooking spray and sprinkle with kosher salt. If you want to get fancy add some Trader Joe's Chile Lime Seasoning Blend (or garlic if you're into that). Bake at 400 for 4-6 minutes, until crispy. You can do this part ahead and store in a Ziploc for several days.

2. Lay chips in a single layer in a 9x13 or sheet pan.

3. Sprinkle with shredded cheese, drizzled queso, and cotija. Top with chicken and bake at 400 until melty (about 5 minutes).

4. Pull out and top with pico, avocado, mango, cilantro, and a drizzle of cilantro-lime ranch. Sometimes I like to top my nachos with tons of shredded lettuce and treat it like an upside down taco salad.

P.S. I had a batch of chips get SUPER dark at 7 minutes and thought they had burned, but they were great. So, don't get too scared if they're really brown and crispy.

When I first wrote this recipe, I was NOT eating with the goal of "fat loss", so my macros were high and this was a normal-sized dinner for me. When I'm cutting, this is heavier than I like. Feel free to build your own meal with just one lavash. Decrease cheese and avocado to lower the fat. I've made these SO light--and they're always still so good!

Feeding the family: Make a second sheet pan decked out for the family with beans and plenty of cheese so they don't come begging for yours.

Meal-prep thoughts: Prep chips, chicken, cilantro ranch, and pico ahead of time. Everything else comes together in minutes.

chicken enchilada spaghetti squash bake

PREP: 20 MINUTES   TOTAL: 45 MINUTES   SAUCE SERVES: 3-4

1 onion, diced (130g)

1/2 bell pepper, diced (70 g)

2 cloves of garlic, minced (or frozen cubes)

1 tsp cumin

1 tsp salt

1 tsp chili Powder

1/4 tsp pepper

4-oz can diced green chilis

1/4 cup +2tbs red enchilada sauce (90 g)

1/2 cup whipped Greek cream cheese (88 g)

1 large cooked spaghetti squash (630 g)

14 oz chipotle-lime taco chicken (400 g)

1/2 cup lite 3 cheese blend (56 g)

NOTES:

Chicken: Both the chipotle-lime chicken and the smoky honey-cilantro chicken would work great in this. Macros would hardly change between the two.

Greek Cream Cheese: If you can't find the Greek cream cheese, use 1/3 less-fat cream cheese. If you add the same 4 tablespoons (which will be 60 g) it will add 1.5 g fat to one serving.

Enchilada sauce: My favorite jarred enchilada sauce (and the one calculated in the macros) is the red bottled one from Trader Joe's!

NUTRITION

Serving size: 350 g casserole with no toppings
316 Cal/8.1F/23.8C/34.2P

Search MFP for:
"Lillie Eats and Tells Chicken Enchilada Spaghetti Squash Bake"

1. Sauté onions and bell peppers over medium heat with cooking spray and a sprinkle of kosher salt for about 5 to 10 minutes (or until tender). Add garlic and cook another minute or 2--careful not to burn.

2. Add diced green chilis, spices, enchilada sauce, and Greek cream cheese to the pan, stirring until melty and warm. Add spaghetti squash and chicken and stir until combined.

3. Spread mixture in a greased 8x8 pan, drizzle with remaining 2 Tbs enchilada sauce, and sprinkle with lite cheese. Bake at 350 for 25 minutes or until the cheese is melted. If you like more color, broil for a couple of minutes at the end. Remember: lite cheese won't get as melty and bubbly as a full-fat option. Garnish with fresh cilantro and a squeeze of fresh lime,

P.S. For a few more macros top with avocado, fat-free sour cream or Greek yogurt, skinny cilantro-lime ranch, and cotija cheese. Pair with a simple green salad drizzled with the skinny cilantro-lime ranch.

It will be a little watery when it first comes out of the oven because of all the moisture in spaghetti squash. It doesn't bother us (it sets up more as it sits). If it bothers you, sauté your squash alone first to cook out some moisture.

Feeding the Family: My older two kids like spaghetti squash, but you could also use the same ingredients to make a second dish with tortillas instead of spaghetti squash for a quick stacked-enchilada casserole.

Meal-prep thoughts: This is a great meal to make ahead of time. I almost liked it better the next day (warmed up in the microwave, you could also throw it under the broiler.)

MACROS 101

A rough explanation from a macro counter (who does not claim to be a macro coach.)

The term "macros" is short for macronutrients. It refers to your fat, carbs, and protein. So far, so good.

Tracking or counting your macros just means you're counting (with the help of a food-logging app like My Fitness Pal) how many grams of those macronutrients you get in a day. Really, it's just a step beyond counting your calories, which, I'll confess I had never done a day in my life, before I decided to dive head first into this.

Calories are still king and having them in the right place for your goals is going to be the most important part of the formula. While trying to lose body fat you'll want to be in a caloric "deficit," meaning that you're eating less than your body burns each day. If your goal is to maintain, you'd ideally be eating just about what you burn each day. If you're trying to build muscle, you'd eat slightly OVER what you burn each day. Still making sense?

Then why not just count calories?

PROTEIN

The breakdown of macros is primarily focused on making sure that a good portion of those calories comes from protein. Proteins are the building blocks of our muscles, and muscles are what make our bodies look PRETTY once we shed the fat we'd hoped to (rather than just being a smaller version of the same shape we've been frustrated with). Hanging on to a new thinner frame is so SLIPPERY when you're not actually doing anything to change your body COMPOSITION. An indulgent weekend, followed by a tip in the scale, and it can feel like all the work has been undone! But with muscle GROWTH, there are so many more changes going on than just the shedding of scale/water weight. Those firm new curves can't be stolen in a weekend.

Muscles are also, of course, what we hope to GROW if we're eating in a surplus. Rather than just love handles! They also help our bodies burn more fat around the clock, thereby creating a higher resting metabolic rate and higher total daily energy expenditure--which is a long way of saying: **more muscle means more food!**

So, if we've got strength or aesthetic goals, muscles are important--and it's hard to build the muscles that firm up our shape without eating enough protein. I'M NOT A FITNESS COACH or a health professional of any kind, but the amount of protein usually recommended for fat loss and muscle growth is about .8 to 1 times your body weight. Some base it more on lean body mass, but this is a simple way to figure out a good protein goal. If you weigh 140 lbs, you might want to try and hit around 140 g of protein. If you have a lot of weight to lose, and, say your goal weight is about 150 lbs, maybe set your protein around that goal weight: 150 g.

CARBS AND FAT

The breakdown between carbs and fat is much more flexible. Some prefer to give more to carbs, some to fat. This can be adjusted according to preference. I prefer these calories being broken down about 60/40 in favor of carbs because I feel like that creates more food throughout the day! Again, this will vary according to preference.

AN EXAMPLE: HOW TO SET YOUR MACROS

So, if you are trying to set yourself some macro goals to help shed body fat, here's a general order of operations:

1. Determine caloric deficit: A good general rule is body weight x 10,11,12,or 13. Adjust your numbers closer to 10 if you're more sedentary and closer to 13 if you're very active and/or have a very fast metabolism.
2. Set protein goal: (Body weight x1) or closer to (goal-body weight x1) for those with more to lose.
3. Distribute the rest of your calories between fats and carbs according to preference. I like 60/40 favoring carbs.

So, as an EXAMPLE:

1. A 140-lb female wanting to shed fat who works out pretty regularly might set her calories at 1680. (140x12)
2. Then, protein at 140. (140x1). Since each gram of protein is worth 4 calories, we know those 140 grams will take up 560 calories. So since 1680-560=1120, we've got 1120 calories remaining to split between fat and carbs.

3. 1120x0.6= **672 calories for carbs** and 1120x 0.4= **448 calories for fat**. Since each gram of carbs is worth 4 calories and each gram of fat is worth 9, we can figure out what a reasonable set of goals might be in grams. (672/4=168 g carbs and 448/9= 50 g fat.)

So this, my very rough and basic example, shows you what a pretty active woman with a current or goal weight of around 140 pounds MIGHT use as her "macros," or daily breakdown of macro nutrient goals: 168 carbs/50 fat/140 protein and 1680 calories.

If these were your goals, it will feel hard at first! It will feel especially hard to hit that protein goal while the carbs are lower. But remember this: when you've shed some of the unwanted fat and are ready to "reverse diet" (or slowly add back in calories to maintain for a while because the calories at which you maintain your weight should not be the same as the calories you use to lose), you'll add mostly carbs! Your protein goal is already sufficient so as you increase carbs, it will get SO much easier to get your protein in without having to work so HARD at it. And, if you've added or increased weight lifting as part of your exercise routine and you're seeing your body composition changing, it will be SO WORTH IT.

Before you know it, you'll be running low on protein by the end of the day and hoarding it just like your precious carbs and fat! (Maybe that's just me.)

HOW TO TRACK (IF YOU WANT TO)

I've always used the premium version of My Fitness Pal, so that's what I know and love. But, you certainly don't have to pay for premium! I just got hooked on a few features it offers. But the free version gets the job done, and there are other apps as well. Currently, all Lillie Eats and Tells recipes with the macros for easy logging, are only available in My Fitness Pal. However, there is most likely some "manual add" feature where you can always log the macros of a meal into your app if you're not on MFP.

When you're logging your own food, you'll go to add something to your diary and you can either search for it, or scan the barcode if it's applicable. You'll want to double check anything before you choose it. There are plenty of errors in the database.

When logging one of my meals, you'll search "Lillie Eats and Tells" plus the name of the meal. You'll want to use the exact title, so follow my instructions on the bottom of each recipe for easy logging!

And, if you don't count or track and just want healthy recipes, great! Covered. You can count on these meals being a very balanced ratio of carbs/fat/and protein for ANYONE--generally lower in fat and higher in protein. Most importantly (to me), you can ALSO count on them being delicious and FILLING.

HOW TO CREATE A RECIPE IN MY FITNESS PAL

Want to alter a recipe? No problem! Just copy the recipe into the "create recipe" feature in MFP to build your own. Make whatever adjustments you need to, then double check each item to make sure the macros make sense.   Scan barcodes when you can, and even STILL, you'll need to double check. I've logged 1000 calories of cilantro before, so, unfortunately, you can't skip this part! There are plenty of wonky options in there.

Now THIS IS THE KEY. If your soup, for example, serves 10, you could put 10 as the number of servings and estimate if you'd like. Or, divide it perfectly in 10ths.   That works too!

BUT-- I much prefer this method:

1. You've entered all ingredients - whatever they were (700 g raw chicken breasts, 2 cans tomatoes... etc.)
2. When the recipe is done, the soup is cooked, the chicken is grilled, casserole out of the oven etc., WEIGH THE FINAL PRODUCT to get it's net weight in grams. (Don't forget to subtract the weight of the dish.) THIS is the number you'll use when MFP asks you how many servings it makes. By doing this, you've assigned just ONE GRAM to each serving, so the macros will look crazy low. Now save it.
3. When you go to weigh your soup, you can put 300 grams in your bowl and log 300 "servings" of your soup. This allows you to have however much you'd like each time, or easily eat the leftovers. It even allows you to make the recipe many times in the future, even doubling or halving it, and continue to use the same recipe to log your grams. Hallelujah.

Thank you to my friends Jarica Watts and Tania Koven
for helping me edit this book!

AND THANK YOU FOR YOUR SUPPORT.
I HOPE YOU KEEP IN TOUCH:

www.lillieeatsandtells.com
Instagram: @lillieeatsandtells
Facebook: Lillie Eats and Tells

I'd love to see your creations on Instagram!
Tag me @lillieeatsandtells and use #lillieeatsandtells